MW01716655

LETTERS FROM A SOLDIER

the wartime experiences of a Canadian infantryman, 1943-1945

LETTERS FROM A SOLDIER

the wartime experiences of a Canadian infantryman, 1943-1945

Robert Miles Sanderson
Marie Sanderson

ESCART PRESS

© Marie Sanderson, 1993

All rights reserved.
No part of this publication may be reproduced or used in any form by any means without written permission of the publisher. Critics or reviewers may quote brief passages in connection with a review or critical article in any media.

Although great care has been taken to trace the ownership of copyright material used in the text (including illustrations), the author and publisher welcome any information enabling them to rectify any reference or credit in subsequent editions.

ISBN 0-9692383-9-8

ESCART PRESS
Faculty of Environmental Studies
University of Waterloo
Waterloo, Ontario
N2L 3G1

Canadian Cataloguing in Publication Data

Sanderson, Robert Miles, 1920-1978
Letters from a soldier: the wartime experiences of a Canadian infantryman, 1943-1945

Letters to the author's parents, Nellie and Stanley Sanderson
ISBN 0-9692383-9-8

1. Sanderson, Robert Miles, 1920-1978 - correspondence.
2. World War, 1939-1945 - Personal narratives, Canadian. I. Sanderson, Marie, 1921-
II. Sanderson, Nellie. III. Sanderson, Stanley.
IV. Title

D811.S35 1993 940.54'8171 C93-094208-6

For

Susan

and

Hardie

and

James

Preface

Almost every family in Canada was personally involved in the Second World War (1939-45). More than one million men and women, one tenth of the country's population, served in the armed forces. More than 630,000 of the Canadians in uniform were in the Army; 74,000 of these became casualties and 23,000 died.

This book is the story of the Second World War as seen through the eyes of an infantry soldier, my husband, and told in the letters that he wrote to his mother and father during the period January, 1943 to June, 1945. I have reproduced the letters, written almost fifty years ago, with only minor omissions of a personal nature. I have added information on the general military situation obtained from historical accounts of the Canadian Army during World War II. As such, it is a pertinent social history of the era.

The manuscript was sent to the late Colonel Fred Tilston of the Essex Scottish regiment who was my husband's commanding officer in Europe. Tilston was awarded the Victoria Cross for his actions in the Rhineland campaign, and certainly is regarded as one of Canada's heroes. He died in 1992, and I am grateful that he wrote:

You have been successful in telling Bob's story by the use of his personal letters to his family. . . His letters to his mother and father tell me that the Sanderson family was a happy one of high principles that were reflected in Bob's high moral conduct.

Your manuscript is a most interesting account of a soldier's personal wartime life experiences and reactions in the Canadian Army in Canada, the United Kingdom, the theatre of war in Northwest Europe and finally as a prisoner of war. It should be published, and it will provide deep satisfaction to those reading it.

Marie Sanderson
Waterloo, 1993

Acknowledgements and Sources

I would like to express my deep gratitude to several people for their information, guidance and encouragement: Rob Meanwell of Windsor (formerly Captain Meanwell of the Essex Scottish Regiment), Jeffrey Preston of Stratford (formerly Major Preston of the Cameron Highlanders Regiment) and especially Walter (Pete) Heaton of Harrow (formerly Private Heaton of the Essex Scottish Regiment), all of whom appear in the book.

Cliff Chadderton, President of the Prisoners of War Association of Canada, and the Directorate of History of the Department of National Defense in Ottawa have kindly helped me in locating sources of information.

I have consulted the following for information on the Essex Scottish Regiment and the Canadian Army in World War II: C.P. Stacey ***"The Canadian Army 1935 - 1945: an Official Historical Summary"*** (1948); W.D. and S. Whitaker ***"Rhineland: the Battle to end the War"*** (1989), and ***"Dieppe"*** (1992); the ***"War Diaries of the Essex Scottish Regiment"*** (National Archives of Canada, Ottawa), and in particular R.W. Meanwell ***"The Essex Scottish Regiment: 1939 - 1945"*** (1946).

Other sources of information include J. Mellor ***"Forgotten Heroes, the Canadians at Dieppe"*** (1975); T. Copp and R. Vogel ***"The Maple Leaf Route": Victory*** (1988) and J.A. Mowbray,

"The Essex Scottish in the Rhineland, 12 January to 10 March, 1945" (M.A. thesis, Wayne State University, Detroit, 1966).

The two original maps were prepared in the Faculty of Environmental Studies Cartographic Centre, University of Waterloo, by Barry Levely.

L/CPL. R. SANDERSON REPORTED MISSING

Word has been received here that Lance Corporal Robert Miles "Bob" Sanderson, son of Mr. and Mrs. H.S. Sanderson of Chesley, has been officially reported as missing in action while fighting on the western front in Holland. The news will be received with general regret in Chesley and throughout the entire district, as he was an exemplary young man in every respect and had a host of friends everywhere. He was one of the outstanding athletes of Bruce County, an exceptionally fine hockey player, having been a member of the High School team and later with the well known Chesley Colts.

He enlisted in March, 1943, while a student at the University of Western Ontario, and trained at Chatham, Ipperwash, Long Branch, Fernie, B.C., and Sussex, N.B., before going overseas. He has been on active service in Holland since November 15, 1944. He was a member of the Essex Scottish Regiment. He has two brothers in the services, Sub.Lieut. Arthur, at Dartmouth, N.S., and L.A.C. Hardie at Clinton, Ont.

1

From Scholar to Soldier

The article on the preceding page appeared in the newspaper ***The Enterprise*** in Chesley, Ontario, on March 3, 1945. The year was the last of the 1939 - 1945 war, and similar articles had appeared in other newspapers, telling the sad news of local army or air force or navy boys who had been killed or listed as missing in action in the war in Europe. Certainly the use of the past tense *"was a member of the Essex Scottish"* was not conducive to optimism on the part of Bob's parents

Robert Miles (or Bob as he was always called) was born in 1920 and was the youngest of the three sons of Nellie and Stanley Sanderson. Three other children—two boys and an only girl—had died in infancy, so the relationship between parents and the surviving children was especially close. Bob's father was the principal of the public school and the choir director in the United Church. He was a stern disciplinarian in school, but at home a loving father with a great sense of humour.

Chesley was, and still is, a pretty little town of some 1,700 people located on the banks of the Saugeen River in Bruce County. It was a great place to be a teenager during the 1930s. There wasn't much money during those depression years, but no one lacked food, and entertainment was cheap. There was a river for skating in the winter and swimming in the summer. As well, there were hockey and football teams. Bob was a good athlete and played football for the school team and hockey for the town's

Chesley Colts as was mentioned in the newspaper article. The churches were the centres of social life, and there were seven of them in Chesley. Everyone went to church on Sunday morning and again in the evening, also on Monday for Young Peoples, and Wednesday for choir practice. Although he rarely spoke of it, or mentioned it in his letters, Bob's religion was important to him and was to be a great source of strength during his army years.

For the Sanderson boys, Hardie, Arthur and Bob, the best times were the summer months. When school was out, the family moved to Inverhuron on Lake Huron where the grandparents, who lived in Pinkerton near Paisley in the early years of the century, had built a cottage. Nellie's sister Florence and her husband Jim Preston from Stratford with their five children lived next door. The two families were very close friends, and there was always lots of fun with all the Preston cousins. For Bob, this lovely Lake Huron shoreline was his favourite place in the whole world.

Teenagers didn't have much chance of summer jobs during the 1930s but Bob was lucky enough to be hired as a counselor at summer camps, first at Camp Ahmek in Algonquin Park where his cousin Jack Preston was a counselor, and then at Camp Keewaydin on Lake Temagami, where he went with his next door neighbour, Fred Stokes, who was the United Church minister's son. Bob was 6 ft. tall and well built and an excellent swimmer and canoeist. His camp experience and "roughing it" was to stand him in good stead during his army career.

In September 1939, the people of Chesley were jolted out of their quiet existence when war was declared between Canada and Germany. Almost immediately, the Department of National

Defence issued a General Order authorizing the organization of a Canadian Active Service Force of two Divisions, composed mostly of existing military organizations. Enlistment was entirely voluntary and many young men from Chesley "joined up" as it was then called. No legislation for compulsory military service was introduced at this time since the Prime Minister, Mackenzie King, was committed to a policy of no conscription for overseas military service because of the strong opposition in the Province of Quebec.

The First Canadian Division, under General Andy McNaughton was sent to England in December 1939 and by February, 1940, the Canadian Army in Britain numbered some 23,000 soldiers. There was no trouble obtaining volunteers, since many young men were unemployed and the Armed Services offered free food and clothing and a chance of adventure.

In May 1940, Hitler's armies occupied the Netherlands and Belgium and in June entered Paris. By June 18th, France had capitulated and there was a distinct possibility that Britain itself would be invaded.

In June 1940, in Canada, the National Resources Mobilization Act (NRMA) was passed, requiring every male over the age of 18 to register for military service, although only volunteers were accepted for overseas service (called "going active"). Those compulsorily enlisted (called NRMA men) could not be sent abroad. Volunteers continued to enlist in large numbers and by the end of 1940, there were 57,000 Canadian soldiers in Britain. However, if a young man was a student at university, or necessary for work on the family farm, registration for military service was deferred.

In Chesley, for most young men whose families had the means, it was assumed that university was the next step after high school. After graduating from high school in 1941, Bob entered the University of Western Ontario in London and enrolled in a science course. His parents wanted him to be a medical doctor, to follow in the steps of his Uncle Hardie who was a doctor in Windsor.

Bob loved university life at Western, which at that time had not been much affected by the war. He lived at Huron College and made many friends. There were parties and football games and he was a star on the University's Mustang football team. He found his university courses difficult, but managed to pass all his courses during his freshman year. Returning for a second year at Western, Bob realized that things were changing. Many of his friends at university were enlisting in the armed forces, most of them as officers. His cousin Jeff Preston had joined the Cameron Highlanders in Ottawa in 1940 and was now a Captain. His cousin Beth Preston had joined the Navy as a nurse and had been posted to Scotland.

In August 1941, Prime Minister Mackenzie King visited the Canadian Army in England and found them impatient to get into action, since they were involved primarily in protecting England's south coast and in training exercises. In Europe, the German conquest had reached its maximum extent with the invasion of Russia. In December, 1941, Pearl Harbour was attacked by the Japanese and the United States entered the war. There was a great deal of pressure from the Russians on Prime Minister

Churchill and President Roosevelt for a second front in Europe.

In March, Lord Louis Mountbatten became Chief of Combined Operations and a raid on Dieppe on the French coast was planned, with the purpose of "hardening" the troops as well as training them. There has been a good deal of controversy about the Dieppe raid and why it took place when obviously it was bound to fail as a "surprise" attack against a strongly defended German port city. For the Canadian Army the raid, which took place finally on August 19th, was a disaster. Some 5,000 Canadian troops were involved and only 2,211 returned to England while some 1,900 were taken prisoners of war. The Essex Scottish Regiment, with whom Bob eventually was associated, took part in the engagement. Of the 553 Essex officers and men who embarked for Dieppe, only 51 returned to England—382 were taken prisoner and 148 were killed. It was a blow from which the Essex took a long time to recover. These were the first Canadian casualties and the news was treated with shock in Canada. The biggest losses were in the infantry division, as always is the case in war, so the pressure was on the recruiting officers to obtain men for the infantry. This was the reason for the tightening up of the regulations with respect to university students, and for any male student failing even one course it meant military service.

As a dutiful son away from home, Bob wrote his parents almost every week and hundreds of these letters were carefully preserved by his mother and have survived these almost fifty years. The first letter we quote was written after the first semester of his sophomore year at Western.

Robert Miles Sanderson before joining the Army, 1942

2 a.m. Thurs., Jan. 7, 43

Dear Mother and Dad,

Haven't had time to write even a line until now, so hope you will forgive me. As a matter of fact it is a very late hour that I'm writing this and maybe I should be in bed.

Have had one exam (Tuesday) and it was rather difficult. Only two questions. Got the first one not too bad but the second wasn't too good. Have Economics Thursday afternoon (to-day). Should do okay in it but they're all hard.

Have you noticed in the papers about students getting the gate for not passing their Xmas exams? I'm working doubly hard (if possible) with that thought. There were 89 at Queen's required to withdraw and enlist in the armed forces, 75 at Alberta—doesn't sound so good!

I'll write more later but I think I'd better try and get some sleep so I can ace that exam to-morrow (or to-day). Thanks for everything at Christmas and New Years. It was wonderful to be home. Maybe I didn't show it so much but it is. There isn't a better Father or Mother anywhere, you know that, don't you? I'm afraid I don't realize it often enough, but I take it for granted.

However I must close for now. Since this is my first letter to anyone in the New Year, I must say that I hope the New Year brings everything you want which includes everything, doesn't it?

Love,

8

Friday, Jan. 15/43

Dear Mother and Dad,

Well, here I am in Stratford [he was visiting his favourite Aunt and Uncle—Florence and Jim Preston]. *I finished my exams Thursday afternoon. On the whole, I found them rather tough, but I'm hoping for the best. I never did find an exam easy, but I've managed fairly well so far.*

I just came in from a show. It sure is wonderful not to have any studying for a few days anyway. It was awful going through those exams with the thought that just one bad one "cooked your goose". Your letter helped bolster my morale. It got so that I was never sleepy at night but it would be hard to concentrate: when I'd go to bed I'd lie awake for a long time, but in the morning, it would take me ages to waken up. I'd be up but yet not awake. Good thing all my exams were in the afternoon!

Love to you both

The news from the university wasn't good—he had failed in one exam and was required to withdraw to enlist in one of the armed forces. After taking numerous tests, Bob found that he was colour-blind, which automatically made him ineligible for the Navy or Air Force. He hoped to be able to take officer's training for the Army, as many of his friends were doing. He felt that he would be considered a failure by his parents and friends if he couldn't be an officer—like Cousin Jeff!

Monday, Jan. 25/43

Dear Mother and Dad -

The news isn't so hot. I found out Wednesday that I can't get down to Brockville through the R.O.T.C. (Reserve Officer's Training Corps). I didn't want to tell you for awhile. Two set backs in a row would be too much especially when they are so important. I wrote a couple of tests down at M.D#1. (Military District) headquarters which would qualify me for Brockville. Gave my life-history and had several interviews. After it was all over one of the officers took me aside and told me that 90% of the officers are coming from the ranks now and that in one of my tests I'd got just under the required mark. Men coming from the reserve units wishing to go to Brockville must get above a certain mark—so, there's the story!

I thought seriously of going home but thought there would be too many people there who would be asking too many questions that I couldn't answer. Things are still indefinite but I think I'll see Jack McDonald in London and find out what unit he thinks would be best for me and the one in which the chance for advancement would be good.

Was going back to London to-day but Uncle Jim suggested that I stay over till to-morrow. However, personally, I don't think very much can be done. I'm still hoping anyway. I'll probably go to London Tuesday and attend to a few things there. Will let you know what happens there and also if Uncle Jim has any more information.

Am afraid I'll need some money to clear up everything at

Western. I may owe a few dollars to Huron College—but it shouldn't be more than a five spot or so. Have to send my trunk down and buy a ticket.

I'll wait for a letter for a few days in case you wish to tell me anything different.

Don't worry about me—I know you are though.

Love from your son

Wednesday, Jan. 27/43

Dear Mother and Dad,

I'm back in the old hole again—London! Uncle Jim phoned me in Toronto and told me Johnny Metras [the Mustang's football coach] *had some information for me that might help me get to Brockville so Monday night I took the 10 o'clock train to London. Tuesday, I saw Mr. Metras and learned all about it. Wednesday, three other chaps and myself followed Mr. Metras's advice and went to Ipperwash Camp* [a Canadian Army base camp on the shores of Lake Huron near Grand Bend] *to see the Commanding Officer there who is Major Emory. I know him well and he is very nice.*

Apparently he is having rather a hard job finding men suitable as officers—as far as educational standards go. He would take us as soon as possible and give us training for a month or so then recommend us for Brockville.

The only catch is—that test that I tried at M.D.#1! Since I've written it, I don't know whether I could write it again or not.

From what I was told here in London, the only way for me to get a commission is to work through the ranks which is exactly what I would do if I went to Ipperwash. Major Emory is going to speak to some of the officers at M.D.#1 here where I had this test and I'll find out Monday.

The test is a very simple one—and I know I could get it all right. It was my physical condition and state of mind after writing those exams and then hearing the result that was to blame for it. Course you can't tell, it may not have been the test at all. It is used as a good answer for many things. Major Emory agrees that there shouldn't be so much emphasis put on this test. He has done a lot for me and I certainly appreciate it all. He was second in command in our R.O.T.C. last year. Maybe you can't figure out exactly all I've said so far but I'll explain more fully when I see you. By the way, I don't know when that will be either. The indefinite state of things makes it hard to tell.

I don't think there was a more disappointed or unhappier person in the world than me with the exam results and the Brockville situation on top of that. I think I've had my share of the bad breaks—surely a good one will come soon.

Bye for now and will write as soon as there are any newer developments—good or bad. You've taken so much now, there can't be any worse.

Love from your youngest

Everyone knew that in the Army there were "officers", who were gentlemen and non-commissioned "men" who weren't officers. Officers wore uniforms which were well tailored and very smart-looking, and "men" wore very coarse thick woolen uniforms, which were not very flattering. The officers ate well-served meals in the officer's mess; the "men" ate from metal trays, without dishes.

Sunday, Jan. 30/43

Dear Ma and Pop,

I am in Stratford this week end. Things are still as I said in my last letter; nothing new to report. I'm going to see a Captain on Monday and will know exactly where I stand. If everything is okay, I shall join up at Ipperwash and then come back to London for my medical and x-rays. Will then come home and wait for my letter from them as to when they'd want me back at Ipperwash. I should have at least about one week anyway. I'm going to phone Aunt Florence about the outcome with this officer in London and she'll phone you.

Uncle Jim phoned a Major Ross here and he said I could write my test again and hopefully get to Brockville. The same system is used here in Stratford as at Ipperwash, so, if I don't go to Ipperwash I may try this Stratford angle. If a call to the army ever comes, try to phone me ahead of time so I'll know.

I have read the letter from Dad and the ones from you and they have really helped me more than you can think. No one like a Mother and Dad when you hit things in life that you just can't figure or understand. Aunt Florence and Uncle Jim too, have been grand and I hope I can repay them someday.

Don't tell anyone of my activities yet Ma, they're still indefinite.

Love from your youngest,

London, March 9/43

Dear Ma and Dad,

This will be just a note to let you know that to-day I had my attestation and am now in the army. I am staying in Huron College to-night again since I am not yet confined to barracks. (C.B.'d) To-morrow I go out at 8 a.m. to have my vaccinations—after which I am C.B.'d for 24 hours—then I get my 48 hour enlistment leave. I doubt if I'll be able to get home with such a short leave, however.

I got a real hair cut yesterday which should last me for some time. I asked my man (my usual London barber) to cut it short and it sure is—but it feels swell.

Hope you two haven't contacted the mumps epidemic yet—and also have had all the experience with the flu for the winter's duration.

It's about suppertime so will close for now.

Love from your youngest
(Buck Private)

14

Sunday March 14/43
Wolseley Barracks
London, Ont

Dear Mother and Dad,

Well, I can now sing the song "You're in the army now, you're not behind a plough" with gusto. I have had my uniform since Wednesday and have had duties of various sorts to attend to. Thursday I was vaccinated and C.B.'d for 24 hours. Had no bad after effects but my arm was sore for a few days.

Friday I had an interview with the Personnel Officer. It didn't last long because I had already had my interview down town. He gave me no promises and placed me in the infantry of the Canadian Army. While I was in the queue waiting to be interviewed, I noticed that each person, although requesting the artillery, or the service corps, or whatever, was assigned to the infantry, so I surprised the officer by requesting the infantry. (He thought I was nuts!) I am not attached to any particular unit. That will come later on. I can see that I'll have my work cut out in trying to get a commission this way. I'll be a pretty disgusted boy if I don't get a chance at Brockville before I go overseas. First impressions that I've made around here about the recruits who are coming into the army at the same time as myself are pretty low. (A very personal comment, you know, and maybe I shouldn't say that). It is a fact anyway that they're a different type from those whom I have associated with. They're not at all like the boys I found at college. They come from all walks of life. I'm hoping I can find someone soon who will make a satisfactory companion—

but I'm in no big hurry for that.

Friday night at 5 p.m., four of us were put on Ordinance Picket duty—which is guarding the Ordinance Building and seeing that no prowlers (unauthorized persons) are around. Never slept all night. On duty two hours and then off for four hours was the arrangement.

I'm on 24 hour duty again to-night, only this is fire picket. We are the fire fighters assigned to look after Carling Heights from 5 p.m. to-night till 5 Monday night. A large number of draftees left Friday—which accounts for our extra duties.

My address is simply Wolseley Barracks, London—my name, too of course. The number and rank aren't necessary, but I'm a private and my Army identification number is A-106266. Will likely be here for over a week.

Hope all is well with you two -

Love

Bob's training as an infantryman began with a transfer to Chatham, Ontario. He still looked forward to recommendation for officer's training, but he began to feel more at home with army life as his April 5th letter indicates.

Chatham
April 5/43

Dear Mother and Dad,

Thursday, at noon, we were shipped down here to

Chatham. The barracks is nicer than the one in London with very well kept grounds and considering everything it should not be too bad for two months. No hills around here. Chatham, of course, was the one camp I didn't want to be sent to, however, in the army you take it and like it!

My leaves are practically useless as far as getting home, I'll just have to put that out of my mind. I get two 36 hour leaves and one 48 hour during my stay here. With distance and the train connections you can see the situation.

In two months I'll be through here and then I'll be sent to Camp Ipperwash so I should be able to get home from there all right.

We've had quite a bit of training so far. They don't waste time in the Active Army. It is all old stuff to me and I find it very easy, but everyone has to go through it—it's called Basic Training!

We rise at 6 a.m. and our personal duties such as washing, shaving, putting bed up, shining shoes and buttons and having exercises as well as breakfast gives us little idle time to be ready for parade at 7.45 [There were lots of route marches and weapons training—with rifles and Sten and Bren guns. As the officers told the infantrymen, their weapons were their best friends].

I don't mind it so much. There are plenty here who hate the life, sorry to say, but the way things were with me, and the way I felt before I joined up, I wouldn't want civilian life back again till after the war.

Love,

#14 Platoon "C" Company
#12 Basic Training Camp
Chatham, Ont

Sunday, April 11/43

Dear Mother and Dad;

It was wonderful to sleep in this morning till 7 a.m. since it's the "Day of Rest" and I look forward to a day without the usual drill, inspections, and orders to obey.

Sunday here is a decided change from all other days, which is as it should be. We all parade to chapel service at 9 a.m. and the Padre looks after us from then until 10 a.m., then we have the rest of the day off to do as we wish. This morning we had the Salvation Army Band to lead us in the old Army hymns and the Padre gave us a sermon on "Courage" and how it applies to soldiers - the same old stuff but he made it fairly interesting.

It's a beautiful day out. It has been quite windy and cool lately (it always is in the morning) but to-day the wind has died down and the sun is shining in the proper spring like manner. It's a day one should go for a walk into Chatham (the camp is on the out-skirts of the city) but the city seems so dead and uninteresting.

Keith Butler is a Lieutenant down here now. He was just moved here from Ipperwash. I was talking to him yesterday. He had quite a bit of difficulty getting his commission too—but he has it! Last time I saw him I had two stripes (a corporal) and he had none. That's the way it goes though! Some chaps are picked out here and made army instructors acting as lance corporals. I hope that doesn't happen to me because I want to get to Ipperwash.

I just found out that I can be made a fully trained soldier in four months by finishing my training at Ipperwash. I could be sent anywhere then. I'm counting on further training at Brockville, but it's going to be a mighty bumpy and crooked road there—but, somehow or other, I'm going to get there.

Have I ever described some of my hut mates? They are an education in themselves. One man who sleeps next to me just got out of the penitentiary (I don't know why he was in) and he's plenty tough—both in appearance and action. His hair has turned gray although he's only 30 and he says life here is Heaven compared to what he's just left. Some of the boys are almost dead when night time comes—but he's ready for anything.

Then there are two Polish men nearby. They quite often get angry at each other and swear at each other in Polish. It's really very interesting to hear and watch these two. Most of the time they do it jokingly so they seldom get too ferocious at each other. One has travelled all over the States with some famous circus so he has some wild stories as well as a terrific vocabulary, in more ways than one. There are a couple of us who still manage to keep our adjectives down to the expressive "darns" and the odd "damns". One or two of the boys in our hut avoid the beer halls but they're very dull company I've found so far—hence I have a great time, usually looking after my so called new comrades. For many of the boys there's nothing in this town to do but go out and get drunk. So, since I don't do that, I have little to do. I haven't found one yet who has my tastes around camp but I seem to get along okay with everyone.

Unless you are known in a city, a private like me has a slim chance of making any female acquaintances that are worthwhile. Some of the boys have a wild time as you can imagine, and it's these few that spoil the name of the Army and the Army private. But social standing in the Army is nil. Either you are a good soldier or you are not and that's what pays off. I've found that out already!

I get my first 36 hour leave next week end. I may go to Stratford but I had planned to go to Detroit and see the sights. I've explained why Chesley is out since 36 hours is too short to get there. I'll be home on May 27 and 28th. I get a 48 hour leave then when training has been completed. The time is going rather fast here and I have no trouble getting asleep once the lights go out at 10 p.m.

I was hut orderly the other day—lasts 24 hours. Keep fire going all night—no sleep but I was surprised how well I got along without it.

Bye for now

As Bob was finding out, the Army private did not have a very good reputation with the general public. In the early years of the war, most of the enlisted "men" had only Grade 7 or 8 education. It was unusual to find a private with a year and a half of university education! But as he was also discovering, there were good soldiers and ones who weren't so good. In battle, he was to find that his life often depended on his companion, and whether he was a good soldier.

Wed. April 21/43

Dear Mother and Dad,

Was great to hear your voices on Sunday. I enjoyed my visit to Stratford very much. Aunt Flo as usual was swell and packed me a lunch to take back with me and I had it Sunday night when I got back to Chatham.

I wore my civvies all the time I was there and it was great to get into soft clothes for a few hours. [The clothing for the Canadian army private was made of very heavy, itchy woolen material and Bob hated it].

Am getting to know my platoon boys and hut mates better each day and the better I get to know them the more I like them. They're really not such a bad bunch. They're sort of rough and tough, some of them, but we have a lot of fun. My new officer is okay too—he's a friend of Keith Butler's. Had a talk with him to-day and he says he'll do all he can for me—so that's something.

Have a slight cold these days but nothing serious. The training is rolling along and to-morrow it will be three weeks that I've been here! It's getting near 9.30 p.m. when the mail leaves, so I'd better hurry. Your last letter was very welcome and I was glad to get it with all your news and comments.

I've been coaxed to join the boxing team since I'm told I have the best build in the platoon [Bob weighed 170 pounds] *and they think I have the makings of a boxer. Will be good experience even if I don't last past the first tournament.*

Am in the choir here too. Was at church Tuesday night—mostly a sing-song.

Must close—Love -

Sunday, April 25/43

Dear Mother and Dad,

Easter Sunday it is! We had our regular chapel service this morning at 9.30 but our books didn't have any Easter hymns so we had the usual ones. To-night I think I'll go to Uncle Jeff's old church. It certainly isn't much like Easter here. The weather is dull and rainy, although yesterday was grand! The trouble was there was nothing to do to make the best of it. Went down town and walked around for a while. Had supper then went to a dance and got back into barracks by 11 p.m.

Another Lieutenant from Western came in this week. I knew him well since he was in my year and left just last fall. We had quite a conflab and he wants me to go to Detroit with him some week end. Used to take lectures with him and quite often we sat together. Makes it rather difficult down here and doesn't make me feel any too happy that I'm not in his position. However give me time and I'll make a better officer with the experience I get here.

Met a girl from Western yesterday and I expect to have a date with her this week. Haven't any idea what to do but might find something. Probably a show.

Am going to buy a Victory Bond somehow or another and pay for my rifle indirectly. Not much news, folks. Make sure you two have a pleasant weeks holidays. Give my regards to the Sanderson family and Prestons if you go to Stratford.

Love and Kisses -

The mention of expenses in the next letter recalls the very

different value of money in those days from that in the 1990s. Bob's pay as a private in the Army was $1.50 per day and he was able to send money home as well as buy a $100 Victory Bond as he explains in the letter of May 2.

Sunday, May 2/43

Dear Mother and Dad,

I was very glad again to get your letter with all the news. By now, you are probably back in the old town and I hope your Easter trip was a very happy one.

You were wondering what I was doing with my money. I'm buying a $100 Victory Bond and if I get a commission I can use it. If not, it goes to Dad for part of the money I owe him.

I have my next 36 hour leave next week. I think I'll go to Detroit. The U.S.O. (a service organization for U.S. Military personnel) there looks after the men in service very well. A private in U.S. is quite different from one over here as far as public opinion is concerned. Everything is free at the U.S.O. so my train fare will likely be my largest expense—about $2.00.

Am saving any extra time I might possibly wring out for my weekend at the end of this month. I'm looking forward to it very much. Will be wonderful to be home again even if it is only for a few hours. I'm going to try and get away on Friday in time to catch the 6.30 train for home at London—but that's doing a lot of hoping.

To-morrow I get my first taste of kitchen work. I'm on all day washing dishes, etc. so I'll have a real time of it. Meals have been very good except that this part of Ontario grows onions far too well. The cook specializes in putting a taste of onion here and there in most of his fancy(?) dishes. They have Spanish onions quite often and the smell of them is enough to make anyone bilious.

Western starts its C.O.T.C. camp to-day. I'll bet there are many more from Western down here or other camps by next fall.

Your loving son,

Bob hated the smell and taste of onions and his mother hoped that the army would change that (but it never did). Bob felt that it was adding insult to injury when, in Chatham, his unit was ordered to the Point Pelee marsh area to build dikes to protect the onion fields from flooding!

Monday May 3/43

Dear Aunt Florence,

Again I was glad to hear my name called and receive a letter from you with all the Stratford news. Mother and Dad will be in Chesley again; I hope they had a successful and happy Easter holiday. I knew they would enjoy themselves in Stratford with your fine hospitality.

Training is rolling along as usual. To-day I was on kitchen duty for the first time—dishes, dishes, and more dishes. What a day! This morning I took time off from kitchen work to go down to *the rifle range for target practice. Our platoon had the rifle range and, my dear Aunt, I did my best to stick out like a sore finger and (lo and behold) I was successful in getting 10 bull's-eyes out of 10, giving me the highest possible score of 50. I was the only one with a perfect score, so I won a 10¢ pool worth $2.00 and also won myself a few names such as "Champ" and "Dead Eye Dick" to add on to my others.*

I was on fire picket Sunday night from 5.30 till to-night at the same time. Thank goodness there were no fires.

I'm expecting to go to Detroit this week-end and on May 28th I get my big 48 hour leave and will be going home then. Am looking forward to it, like a kid looks forward to Christmas.

Love,

Tuesday, May 11/43

Dear Mother and Dad,

My thoughts were with you Ma, on Mother's day, even though I was in the thriving city of Detroit on that day. I was going to phone, but I thought I'd save my money and if there was any left when I once more got to Canada, I'd do it then. I was hut orderly to-day (and night) and that kept me within the confines of the hut, so again I couldn't phone, however to-morrow I shall. Even though I was in the States I wished I could have been home last week end especially for that day. I miss seeing my Mom and Pop very much. I don't think I need to tell you how much I think of you, Ma, you know, but the older I get the better I see how well you have looked after me and how much you have done for me—and hence the word Wonderful does not even do you justice. You can be included too Dad!

My week end turned out swell. Although it started and ended with rain, the weather was O.K. for it cleared up before the afternoon was half over. Sunday was ideal.

Got into Detroit about 4 in the afternoon and proceeded to the U.S.O. where we were wonderfully received. "We" means about seven of us from Chatham. The U.S.O. is a grand place, really. There is something going on there all the time. The hostesses are on the job all the time and see that we don't have time on our hands while in the U.S. Everything is free. (By the way, the hostesses are all young and I don't know how it is that practically all are very smart looking too). But that's beside the point. Free meals, free lodging and free cigarettes, etc. etc. I slept in a dorm opposite the Fox theatre just off Woodward.

Sat. May 15

That's as far as I got early Tuesday morning. I got too tired to write and since then I've been pretty busy. Tuesday night I phoned you and it was sure great to hear your voices. I went to a show after I had phoned you and got back to camp just at 10 p.m. Wednesday I went down town and got a hair cut. Went up to the Service Club for awhile then back to camp. Thursday night six of us went to Blenheim to make arrangements for our platoon party at a hotel there. I'm on a committee of four to help arrange it—cars, eats and of course—beer, for those who want it and it is practically unanimous for that. There are a couple of us who still prefer cokes. I had to drive the car back from Blenheim that night. Four got pretty high so another chap from Wiarton and myself had to look after them. It's not the first time I've had to do that. [Bob's parents were rather strict Methodists, so alcohol was always taboo in their house].

Last night I went to a party at the service club for awhile. Dancing and singing. Very nice collection of girls but the floor was too small and we couldn't dance.

I tried to get a 2 o'clock pass for to-night so I could get to a dance to-night but I didn't get it. This morning I've had a 10 mile route march so I guess I'll be in better shape to-morrow by coming in at 11 p.m.

Got paid to-day. They gave me $10. I paid $1 for the platoon party; $1 to a chap who had loaned me that sum previously; 50¢ for another platoon party that I was invited to next Monday (to-morrow). Ours is Wednesday of this week. Then Saturday afternoon (I'm finishing this on Sunday afternoon) I went down town and bought a pair of long summer pants for my summer issue. They only give us short pants and we can't wear those heavy boots to dances, and those putties are too hot for summer days—so I squandered $2.95 on a pair. Then last night I went to a show and had supper down town so you can see how that pay went. I'm afraid I'll have to get $5 out of the bank to get home because we don't get paid again till after our leave at the end of May.

I've heard nothing about an N.C.O. (non-commissioned officer) course here. I really don't want one till after I finish my advanced training at Ipperwash. The training here is so simple and routine. At Ipperwash I would have the experience of being a fully trained Infantry man and otherwise I would miss that. I'm pretty sure I can get one there. Major Emory is back there now. However, if I'm offered one here I'll find out if it's possible to let it go till after my advanced training. I know one thing now, and that is that they've no better private in the infantry than myself right now. I'm not conceited, I'm really twice as good as I think I am, as one of my friends always says! Guess that's the part that counts even if I am unfortunate about a commission.

I've been coming along very well in my training. There are less than two weeks to go now, then our Basic will be completed. I've scored 100 in my two times on the rifle range; 50 both times and that is a perfect score. No one in my platoon had that score or above 90 so I'm quite proud of that. Haven't heard of anyone doing that well in any other platoon, but undoubtedly there are some. Have had small simple tests in other parts of our work, but they have been oral and no difficulty was encountered.

It's turned out very warm and windy to-day. I slept till 4 this afternoon. Was quite tired for some reason or other. My weight is 170 so I'm keeping about the same.

Oh yes, my Detroit week end! Sunday I toured Detroit on the buses for free. It was a swell day and saw the sights. Sunday night I was at the U.S.O. and met some new girls, danced and went to one of the girl's places for a spot of lunch before I caught the train. She likes our Canadian uniforms too, she says, but I don't know why. Phoned Uncle Hardie at Windsor. Told him I'd write him. Must get ready for supper and then church to-night at

Uncle Jeff's old church.

Love

Bob was probably unusual in the Army in his church-going. But he came from a church-going family (his grandfather was a Methodist minister) and he felt strange *not* going to church on a Sunday.

May 21/43

Dear Mom and Dad,

This will just be a note if you don't mind. I'm absolutely out of money, so I'm enclosing a cheque for you to cash for me. I didn't want to do this, but I have to get home and our pay comes at the wrong time. You can send it in your next letter—Monday if possible. I'm trying to leave on Thursday so I can be home Thursday night. Here's hoping anyway.

Yesterday we went to Cedar Springs to the Rifle Range where I got 18 points out of 20. Got three bulls eyes. Some soldiers did not even hit the target! I figure I'm the best shot in the platoon! When I meet up with my first Nazi I'll have confidence in myself anyhow. He'd better run.

Only one more week of training here—then??? I hope I can get to Ipperwash before I take the N.C.O. (non-commissioned officer) course.

Well, be seeing you soon,

All my luff

June 2/43

Dear Mom and Dad,

This is just a note to let you know I returned to Chatham safely and on Tuesday morning I left with about 125 others and landed here in Ipperwash at 5 p.m. Marched in from Stratford with a grand rain coming down and the mud welcoming us.

So you see I'm at advanced training now and no N.C.O. opening as yet. I'm with a good bunch here so I'm happy. The ex-Mountie is my bed-mate so he's a swell partner.

One of the other kids from Western that missed his test is in this platoon too. He's no further ahead than myself so that's something. He's been here in Ipperwash all this time.

It's just a mess of mud all round here and with the heavy rains lately it's terrible. It was really bad to-day but we started right in with our training. Am I ever tired!

We train two nights a week 6.30 to 9 so that we get a special week end every two weeks and I'm lucky. I get one this week end, so I'm coming home I expect on the late train on Friday if all goes well.

Must go now and work -

Love

Private Sanderson at Ipperwash Camp, 1943

Mon. June 7/43

Dear Mother and Dad,

In Ipperwash again, folks and I made it on time. First of all, in my hitch-hiking I was exceedingly lucky. I got a ride from Chesley to Mildmay and waited there for 15 minutes then a lovely big Cadillac zoomed up and picked me up. They were Mr. and Mrs. H. John Krug of Kitchener and they were on their way home from Port Elgin. They insisted on taking me to their place for awhile and I said Okay—since I wasn't expected anywhere at any particular time and I had nothing to lose.

I made quite a hit with their 12 year old daughter and I knew quite a few people that they did so we had a good time. They have a lovely home on Queen Street and they invited three very smart looking girls over to entertain me (their 12 yr. old daughter went to bed early) so you can see I had a swell time. They wanted me to stay at their place over night but I thought I had imposed on them enough (supper too) and caught the bus for Stratford at 11 p.m. Just saw Uncle Jim and Jack when I went to bed and in the morning when they drove me to the station so I haven't much news there. Aunt Flo is still up at the lake.

The train for Ipperwash left at 8.15 and got here at 10.30. Finished the ride from Thorold by truck. Seven of them were waiting for us. It was one more swell weekend for me and it makes the training go better when you can look forward to another. The sandwiches were scrumptious and I'm nibbling at the cookies bit by bit. Ma, you are wonderful. And Dad, thanks a million for the use of the car to go to Hanover and also for helping me on my way back to Walkerton.

Well, this is just a note as you see, letting you know I'm safe at camp once more—sort of down to earth again and reality. It's not a pleasant feeling coming back to camp after a happy week end but that's life right now.

Thanks for everything, bosses and I'll be seeing you again soon.

Love from your youngest

A-106266 Sanderson R.M.
#3 Company #1 Platoon
Camp Ipperwash,
Forest, Ontario

Monday, June 28/43

Dear Mother and Dad,

Last week was one of our toughest so far—it was tough! The long hours, the training and the hot weather really took it out of me but I'm still perking. My 20 mile route march was a real scorcher. I had a bath in my own perspiration but it didn't cool me off. It ran in a continual stream into my eyes which is not particularly pleasant but four of us went a mile down to Ipperwash Beach and had a swim. The water was grand and I stayed in for a good long time. My mountie friend was down with us and wants me to teach him to swim, so I may satisfy his wishes. He thinks I do ok in the water so I told him it was the Inverhuron stroke that I had attempted to master to some degree of perfection.

To-day I have a spot of pleasant news. I'm writing this while awaiting an interview for the S. of I. which means the School of Instruction. It is an N.C.O. course taken by all ranks and a step forward toward my goal if I get it. I'm not sure what it's all about right now so maybe I'd better wait and tell you after my interview is over.

(Later...) It's over. If all is ok with the officers here after further talk among themselves I'll go to London for another interview with some of my officer friends there then if it's ok, to Three Rivers I go, then if ok, to Brockville and to Ipperwash again with my commission. Got to close. Hope this develops into something.

Love and kisses,

Bob's hope for officer's training was not to materialize. He had numerous promises and several times during his training in Canada was made Lance Corporal (one stripe) Corporal (two stripes) or Sergeant (three stripes) but it seemed that each time he returned to Ipperwash he was demoted to the rank of private.

Meanwhile in Europe, in July 1943, after a long wait, the Canadian Army was involved in action, in the Allied assault on Sicily, with the object of knocking Italy out of the war. By the end of the Italian campaign, 91,000 Canadians had served in the Mediterranean war and of these 25,000 became casualties, and 6,000 died.

In 1943, the Canadian government agreed to send to

Britain 232,000 soldiers (all ranks) plus replacements of 5,000 men per month beginning in September, 1943. It must be remembered that the fighting divisions, the parts of the army at the "sharp end" of battle, the ones actually fighting, were only the smaller portion of the army. An infantry division numbered some 18,000 soldiers, yet the total manpower required to keep these in the field was about 40,000. These included artillery men, engineers, and supply and service personnel.

Bob's letters to his parents rarely mentioned the war. He knew that they—like all parents—heard enough from the radio and reading the newspapers. At least there was no television in those days to bring the horrors of war into everyone's living room. Mostly his letters told of his everyday activities—his hopes for officers training and, of course, his anticipation of leave to see his family. His love for his family certainly came through in his letters.

Tuesday night, July 6/43

Dear Mom and Dad,

I hoped to write you Monday to let you know I'm back at Ipperwash once more and down to business already. This is going to be a busy week I can see. Tuesday morning we had reveille at 4 a.m. and went out to the range and fired our Bren guns. Worked all afternoon and evening till 9:15. To-day we are duty platoon, so we were up at 5:45 and I've been pearl diving (dish-washing) all day. Have a few minutes off this afternoon in between meals so I'm writing you. To-night we have duties till 9 p.m., then we all attend some program in the drill hall—so it'll be late to night again. To-morrow we have another 20-miler so we have to get up at 4 a.m. again. Boy, what fun! Saturday we get up at 4 a.m. and go down to the range to fire rifle, Bren, Sten, and the Tommy guns. To top all this off, we are duty platoon on Sunday!!!

Thursday Route march over! We were back from a 22 mile march by 11 a.m. We had a road show from Detroit U.S.O. last night so we didn't get to bed till 12 p.m. They gave us the afternoon off for sleeping and boy did we use it to advantage.

After the route march five out of our platoon were paraded over to the company commander for an interview to attend the School of Instruction here which will begin shortly. It is a four week course, of very tough work after which you get one stripe as an instructor. (S. of I. is taken by all N.C.O.s and officers.) This is a recommendation from my advanced training here at Ipperwash. The other interview was from my work in Chatham and from my general qualifications. This doesn't mean that I don't go down to Three Rivers before I take the S. of I. course. If I don't go to Three Rivers after my advanced training, I'll be taking the S. of I. course anyway, that part is certain.

Sometimes two months as an N.C.O. instructor has to be served before going to Three Rivers. I don't know whether I can get out of this or not. I hope so.

It's getting late so I'll sign off for now.

Love -

The letters also acknowledged family events. Brother

The three Sanderson sons with their mother

Hardie had enlisted in the Air Force and had also gotten ma... The big family news in July of 1943 was the birth of the Sandersons' first grandchild, a girl!

Sun. July 11/43

Dear Mother and Dad -

Greetings and salutations to the new grandparents! I got a card from Hardie giving me the news of the grandest baby ever—according to Hardie. Now I can inform the boys in the platoon that I am to be henceforth known as "Uncle Bob". Long Stuff (the ex-Mountie) calls me that now—when he doesn't call me something else.

I had an interview with my company commander and until I hear from the interview with those other officers about Three Rivers I'll take the School of Instruction course. It's a four week course and tough as it can be. The course should be starting soon because the last S. of I. school just finished and I'm in the next one —the ex-Mountie is in it too.

To-day (Sunday) I was on duty as a Provost all day until 9 to-night. I rode around with Slim in a jeep—in style. Those little jobs certainly can plough through everything on earth—except water.

I've had a very busy week and next week promises to be the same so I'll be ready for my week end at Inverhuron.

Your youngest sends his love

Wed. Aug. 11/43

Dear Mother and Dad,

As usual I have been very busy "playing at war" since I've come back and I'm trying to sandwich a letter in between parades. I have to go out at 8.30 to-night on a peculiar scheme. We are imagining ourselves as prisoners escaped from a German prison camp. We are taken to some distant point (where, we don't know) and told to meet at camp again at a certain hour. It doesn't matter how we get back as long as we do. It promises to be interesting. Last night we got in at 1 a.m.

(That's as far as I got last night.) To-day, Thursday, was another interesting day. We did battle drill all day including river crossing. There is a great deal to know and it's difficult to remember the various commands for the different formations. We have to-night off so I'll be in bed early. The weather has made practically all of us a tired bunch. Yesterday was the worst though. Last night as I said earlier in the letter we had some fun. They dumped us out about 10 miles from camp (we learned later) and the Captain told us to find our way back to camp by 6 in the morning. Three of us went together and got back about 12.30. (We had left at 9). We visited a few farmers, got a bite to eat here and there, got chased by some steers (and I mean chased!) got some lovely apples, hitch-hiked part of the way, visited at Ravenswood and got a cake and some cookies; in general it was paradise compared to the work we had all day.

There is a chance that my week end will be cancelled. We will all be sent to the companies in the training centre which we left when we entered the S. of I. (School of Instruction). There we will be instructors until the reports come back from London as to where and what we will do next. No one seems to know the full story on this so we'll just have to wait and hope for the best.

Will let you know of any new developments down here as soon as I can. I'll be glad when next Friday rolls around and this course is over.

Love from your youngest -

As Bob indicated in this letter, after his school of instruction course, he was sent back to Camp Ipperwash to be an instructor and this was to be his main role in the Army for almost a year. Perhaps unfortunately for his army career, he was very good at instructing!

Camp Ipperwash

Sat. Sept. 18/43, 1 a.m.

Dear Aunt Florence,

I'm in charge of a picket to-night, so I have time to catch up on some of my letter writing. To-day we had a 22 mile route march and to-night till 6 a.m. in the morning I have this picket duty. Rather tired but I have to-morrow morning to sleep.

I'm back in my old platoon instructing so all is going along as expected so far. Just have to keep in there and hope for the best. Things are in control here anyway and I have a grand bunch of men so I can't ask for anything more than that. I'm the only Corporal in my platoon and in the hut so I have lots of work to keep me occupied. The questions start at 6 a.m. and end at 10.15 p.m. (only when lights are out.)

Have to change the guard so bye for now, and thanks for everything again.

Love from your nephew - Bob

Mon. Oct. 3/43

Dear Mother and Dad,

This morning I got rid of most of my boys to the trained soldier company so now the hut is barren, cold and quiet as I write to you in my little cubicle. I've about five men left and they'll leave to-morrow to go to the Specialist Company for a month or so.

I'm the only N.C.O. in camp to-day. The Mountie gets married next week so he's in London for the day getting things ready. All the others are on week end passes. Some just left to-day and won't be back till Wednesday. All the men will be out of our company by to-morrow and another bunch will be in very soon. Our week ends may be changed to the other week now but mine will likely be the same. I'll be in camp still while the rest of camp is on week end in the future.

Last night I had a great experience—one which I hope doesn't happen very often. It'll take too long to explain it all but one of my men had a few bottles of beer and came back into the hut with some other boys. (He wasn't drunk though.) He was playing around, and he fell and hurt his spine which had been bothering him for some time. He'd been in the hospital for it. It put him into a coma of some sort, then he started to quiver and shake. He threw two men away like flies, ripped his bed apart, also his duffel bag. He was in this state for two hours. Forgot to mention that he kicked two holes in the wall—no one could hold him. (He's 6 feet tall, 175 pounds and 20 years old) Really a good kid too. I took his pulse while he was in the coma and it was 120! As soon as I took the pulse I sent a man for the M.D. who was drinking in the mess. He never came for the corporal, the Orderly Officer, or my sergeant—but he finally came when my company commander ordered him to. Boy, I sure was mad and so is everyone else. We made a report on it and it's about time something was done because he has done the same thing before. He got here just when this kid came out of his spell—two hours after we'd asked him. He wouldn't go to the hospital last night so we had two men looking after him all night. The nervous reaction from it kept the boys busy till 3.30 or so though. He was tossing in his sleep, calling out for his mother, etc. It was quite an evening. Then I was up at 5.30 this morning since I'm C.O.S. (Company Orderly Sergeant) to-day—naturally since I'm the only N.C.O. in camp.

Must close for now

Love -

Mon. Oct. 7/43

Dear Mother and Dad,

Just a note before dinner! Saturday three of us (N.C.O.s) decided to go to Port Huron. Our ride back was assured. We were to meet the chap with the car at the bus depot in Sarnia at 12.30 Sunday morning—but things didn't work out that way. We missed the last bus from Port Huron to Sarnia, not knowing it left at 12 so we started thumbing to the bridge. We walked half way over the bridge—consequently when we reached the bus depot in Sarnia—he had left. We tried thumbing to camp in the snow (snow in October!) and rain but no luck at all. So, we went back to Sarnia and inquired at a taxi office how chances were of hiring one to get to Ipperwash. We had to wait till 3 a.m. before the taxi driver would leave because things were slack for him then. We pooled all our resources and one fellow's watch as security and the taxi got us back to camp at 5 a.m. It was an expensive trip for all of us and we're all without funds. We didn't turn our passes in and fixed it up in the morning (one advantage of being an N.C.O.!). This camp is certainly situated in a lonely barren spot. I've decided that week ends are the only times to leave it. We had a good time at the U.S.O. at Port Huron but the last part of the evening spoiled everything.

Now you can see why I need a few dollars for my week end this Friday—I'm busted. I don't know whether I'll make home this time or not. I may go only to Stratford.

My Victory Bond will be paid in full at the end of this month, so I'll tell them at the pay office to send half my pay to you.

It's time for dinner so I'll end this for the time being. May be seeing you this week end. Look after yourselves.

Love from your youngest

Thursday night, Oct. 14/43

Dear Mother and Dad,

No doubt you are finding things rather quiet this week with just the two of you looking after the homestead. Mother, make sure you take advantage of these days and rest as much as you can. Last week end was grand having the whole Sanderson family all together again. Too bad we couldn't have had a longer visit but guess we should be thankful for even a short one.

Sorry I've been so slow in writing, but with these new men and the "zombies", [This was the term that the regular army men called the "NRMA" soldiers] *we all have a lot of work and the ambition for writing letters is very low (a rather lame excuse though).*

We had a big inspection to-day. Col. Ralston, (our defence minister, you know) was here, so we put on a big show for him. We were on parade all morning. He inspected the whole camp and gave us a short talk. He was dressed in his usual attire— homburg hat and dark suit. This afternoon I gave a few rifle tests to my zombies and men!

I hope this work of mine will smarten up a bit. It's ok. but unless I get a chance at the officers' course I'll be pretty disappointed. Unless I get a commission in this man's army I'll be pretty disgusted with myself. Working with some of these men that I have to is certainly very repulsive at times—but—the army takes everyone and I suppose that's one of the tests of my proficiency in the little job I have.

I got word to-day though that I'm taking a course at Long Branch (outskirts of Toronto) at the end of this month, so it'll be a change and I'll be glad of it. It will be a specialist course on gas lasting three weeks or so. It will prove beneficial to me as an instructor and also for my own good.

There are still no more promotions in the army in Canada as yet. The men who come out of the S. of I. now are only paid private's pay and are not given any stripes. I should have had my second stripe before this.

Love from the Soldier Sonny

Nov. 2/43
Long Branch Ontario

Dear Mother and Dad,

Sorry I'm a day late or so in getting my weekly news bulletin away to you, but there's quite a bit of activity on my part in getting settled in the new course down here at Long Branch, and being near to Toronto doesn't make it any easier for writing letters either.

The course is shaping up into a very interesting one and I'm liking it very well. It's a return to school practically for a great deal of our time is taken up with lectures and in giving lectures ourselves. I have to give five of them during the three weeks down here. The instructors are very good and know their work (all sergeants and officers).

Saturday morning we had lectures, and then in the afternoon, a couple of other N.C.O.s and myself went to the double header football game, which we really enjoyed, then at night, the four of us went to the hockey game. Quite a day! My first professional hockey game—and I was rather unimpressed with the show. My desire is satisfied now. I don't expect to see another for some time.

I hope you are feeling better now mother. Being in the army makes you appreciate parents and home, more than you think.

I'll be seeing you soon

Love -

During 1943, the Canadians were involved in the Mediterranean campaign and one success followed another. By the end of the year most of the Italian peninsula was in Allied hands. The Italian campaign was considered a success because it deprived Germany of its chief ally and allowed the Allies the use of the Mediterranean sea.

Nov. 6/43
Long Branch, Ontario

Dear Mother and Dad,

I'm hoping to get to Stratford this Saturday. I just found out to-day that I'm not on fire picket so I should be able to make it. I'll start hitching at 12 noon.

The course is going along smoothly. My lectures seem to be okay. No one gives a better one, (my opinion of course), and I'm improving each time so I'll be an ace on chemical warfare by the time this course is over.

It's very interesting so I like it not too badly. The work from now on is all new so that makes it even better. Had some tear gas experience to-day, so I was doing plenty crying for awhile. To-morrow we get a gas that has no bad effects but makes you sick. I hope I don't get sick until after I've got my face piece off. The last time I didn't feel too badly after it was over.

Well, I've got a bit of work to do so I'd better get it done while I'm in the mood.

I'll be seeing you this Saturday I hope.

Bye for now,

Many of the Canadian soldiers were given this chemical warfare training, but luckily, none were required to put it to use in Europe. Most didn't carry the gas masks they were issued. It was just another thing to carry.

Tues. Nov. 22/43

Dear Mother and Dad,

Guess you've been wondering if I've hurt my hand in my P.T. (Physical Training) course so soon, but it's really okay. I expected to see you last week end, but Thursday after I had finished my chemical warfare exam (which was easy) I reported to the orderly room on request and I was given orders to stay and take the next P.T. course. It was quite a surprise, but the more courses I can get, the better it is for me. I had all my stuff packed and ready to go home Friday morning, but as you see, it didn't turn out that way.

The gas course was very good. The instructors knew their work and knew how to put such a subject across with the proper enthusiasm. Everyone else returned to camp and three others came up from Ipperwash. A lieutenant (a rugby player of Western that I know well) and another corporal who was in Dieppe, all came down for the course on "Theory of Instruction".

This P.T. course is going to be plenty rough and tough. It'll put me in excellent condition and the work is interesting and quite a bit of it new to me so I think I'll like it okay. If others can take it, I can. We have obstacle training every Monday, Wednesday and Friday afternoons and they make the course what it is (tough, I mean).

This course finishes two weeks from Thursday. It's my odd week end for a leave, but I'm hoping they'll be nice and give me one anyway, so I can get home.

Love

Mon. Dec. 14/43

Dear Mom and Dad,

Before you are too shocked with the more than usual atrocious writing, I'd better explain—my right thumb is in a cast. I broke it. I broke it first in Long Branch on the P.T. course and I had to have it taped so I could finish the course, however, when I came back to Ipperwash, I fell out of a truck. They took a couple of x-rays of it and put it in a cast on Saturday.

My week end as you have gathered was cancelled. I had no money to phone you so I couldn't. Went to Stratford on Thursday night and came to Ipperwash on Friday morning. Slept on the chesterfield at Prestons on Thursday night—only a couple of hours. Aunt Florence said she was writing you so I hope you heard in time on Saturday not to expect me that day.

I was really disgusted with things when I found out I had to report on Friday. They were very short of N.C.O.s so I had to come. Am glad the P.T. course is over but I feel the better for it. Know how to box, wrestle, climb ropes, use unarmed combat, run 3 1/3 miles without killing myself, cross a river on ropes and so on.

When I returned I found that I had qualified on my chemical warfare course with a Q.I. which is the best any of the Ipperwash men got in the chemical warfare course, including the officers, so I'm quite pleased with myself. The two sergeants and one officer were next to me with Q.II.s.

I have been informed that I'll be going to Vernon, British

Columbia for a commando course. I hope this course is as good as the chemical warfare one.

Sunday I was Battalion Sergeant (24 hours) so I couldn't write then—thumb and all. I got off duty at 6 this morning. An officer and I were the big boys on Sunday and we saw that all in the camp was running smoothly. The orderly officer and I had a pleasant time— particularly about 3 in the morning when we made the rounds—Boy, it was really cold, windy and snowy. I'm back in number three company but there are a new bunch of men in and they're a good lot compared to the decrepit zombies who were here when I left.

I'm definitely not getting Christmas off, but New Years. I'll leave here probably on Dec. 29th and have five days, I believe. It's been about three months since I've had a decent week end to get home. If I get it I'll be home on the train on Friday night. I'm not worrying about getting back right now.

I'll sure be glad to get home and see you this week end. Toronto's all right for the odd week end but it's nothing like home. It was a nice change to be at Long Branch but I'm rather glad to be back at Ipperwash. It's really a wonderful camp when you compare it with others. None better!

Bye for now; my address is the same but note the corporal.

Love

By the end of 1943, it was evident that the invasion of Europe was being planned. General Eisenhower was appointed in supreme command of the Allied Expeditionary force for the invasion and his military commander was the British General Montgomery who left the Mediterranean theatre of war to take command of the troops preparing for the invasion. Both Eisenhower and Montgomery reached England in January 1944. The code name given to the invasion was "Overlord".

Back in Canada, Bob was taking a battle drill course in Vernon, B.C. This was the first time Bob had ever been outside Ontario in Canada. And since his parents also had never been west of Ontario, he described his trip for them.

Vernon, B.C.
Friday noon. Dec. 31/43

Dear Mother and Dad,

Here I am at Vernon, B.C. It's quite a place—nestled in a valley surrounded by the high Rockies. They are lost in the clouds to-day and it is a grand sight! We came C.N.R. and it was a wonderful trip, although I'm plenty tired of trains. There were several short stop overs along the way, so we hopped off and looked around.

The trip through Northern Ontario was rather dull. The bush and lakes looked like home to my eyes and I was wishing for summer time and my little canoe. Stopped at Nakina and Hornepayne and was it ever cold with tons of snow everywhere! When we woke up next morning we were in Manitoba—no snow—and flat country with the odd forest here and there. We dragged ourselves away from Winnipeg and headed straight out into the prairies. This was very boring and uneventful with just the flat prairies on all sides to see. The third morning we woke up in Alberta. We had passed through Saskatoon during the evening and left Saskatchewan behind. Very mild in Saskatchewan and no snow!

After leaving Edmonton at noon or so we headed for B.C. and at 5 p.m. we began to see the Rockies. Boy, they're wonderful. The train follows the river most of the way and the Rockies go towering up on both sides of the track. Really a wonderful sight. Went through a few tunnels before we reached Jasper Park, where we had a stop over. Saw some mountain goats and saw as much of the place as I could. You've probably got my card I sent to you by now.

Got dark so we slept through the best part of the scenery in the mountains. We got into our berths at Pine River and went to Kamloops and then to Vernon, getting there about 10 a.m. Right now we're in the camp at Vernon, but to-morrow we go out to our camp (for our particular course) at Coldstream about 6 miles from here. Out there is where we get into tents for five weeks. Some fun! There is quite a bit of snow here, but the weather is rather mild. I hope it doesn't get any colder.

Most of the boys aren't looking forward to their battle drill course—but I am! They're here only because their unit ordered them to go.

Think I've told you most of my trip and the situation of the camp out here. There'll be some things I've forgotten but it'll be in another letter. There are 50 officers and 50 N.C.O.s in the course I'm on. They came from all across Canada so I'll be making new friends from all parts of Canada. The ones I've met so far seem like very good chaps so I think I'll like my stay here. I'm hoping to get out to Vancouver before I leave, but I don't know whether I'll have the energy or the time.

Better give you my address.
A-106266 Sgt. Sanderson R.M.
Battle Wing, S-17 C. S. of I.
Vernon, B.C.

Bye for now—Happy New Year

The "Battle Drill" that Bob spoke of was intended to teach all ranks to appreciate a battle situation and to inoculate the soldier against the fear and unexpected circumstances of actual battle. Everything was done at top speed and the drill was repeated over and over again. It was expected that the tactics of team play, usually carried out while live ammunition was fired over the soldiers' heads, would become automatic to the infantrymen. Actual weapons training, with the Bren gun, known officially as a light machine gun, or the Sten gun, called a light machine pistol, or grenades occupied much time also. Bob was a good shot with his rifle, as he told his parents, but also with a Sten gun, which was fired from the hip. It was a 28 pound light machine gun that could fire 120 rounds per minute and had an effective range of 500 yards. Bob became an expert with the Sten gun, a 9 mm machine pistol of British design, preferring it to the heavier Bren gun. He was to find that in actual battle, some members of an infantry platoon were designated as Bren gunners, while others carried either the standard Lee-Enfield rifle with bayonet or the Sten gun. Bob usually carried the Sten gun.

Jan. 7/44
Dear Mother and Dad,

Things are rolling along here ok. I'm learning lots of battle tactics and it looks like a really good course. It's tough, of course, and I'll be sort of glad when it's finished. It's what I wanted, but I don't like this snow and cold weather. We live in tents which are rather chilly but a cup of hot coffee at breakfast thaws you out and then the old familiar feeling of living comes back. Really glad when the day is done and we get warm again.

The battle course has a separate camp outside of Vernon. There are trucks going into Vernon every night for any activities there, but practically everyone "hits the hay" early and glad to do so.

There are three platoons of officers and one of N.C.O.s and mine—which has officers and sergeants. In mine we have one paratrooper, one American and one airforce officer as well as infantry and articling officers—so you see we have lots of variety here. There are three sergeants who flew up from Jamaica for the course. They find the weather quite different, I can tell you.

I find the air thin here. The elevation is rather high, and after a run it takes quite a while to get your breath back to normal —Guess the snow makes it harder too.

It's really beautiful country , if there was only time to look around and appreciate it. Running over the sides of mountains doesn't increase your love for them to any great extent—but they are nice to look at. There are plenty of deer, pheasants, and coyotes and also the odd bear. I've seen some of these and I heard a coyote howl last night. Quite a mournful sound!

I'm tired and it's 10 p.m. and that's bad. Will write again later. Not much to say—other than this is certainly a realistic camp in all ways—nothing but earnest training going on here. Had a private talk with our O.C. (Officer Commanding) here—a Brigadier Gregg (V.C. winner in last war) a nice chat about the course and Ipperwash.

Love—your youngest

Bob always had a well developed sense of humour, and Army life seemed to strengthen it. He often said that running around those mountains so many times in the same direction had made one leg shorter than the other. He was also learning to "rough it" and to put up with what earlier he would have considered impossible situations, like sleeping in a tent in sub-zero weather! Without doubt, this ability helped him in actual combat situations in Europe.

Sun. Jan. 22/44
Vernon, B.C.

Dear Mother and Dad,

Was swell to get your letter too mom, with all its news. It's amazing how much time you spend in writing letters. I'm finding that out particularly out here. We have quite a bit of night work and besides all this I'm playing hockey for the camp so I'm a busy boy and definitely sleep well at nights—also sleep in as late as possible in the mornings too. I have things organized well in the mornings and every minute is on schedule before our first morning parade. Our hockey team has been doing fairly well lately. We're known as "The Commandos" and there's no doubt about it, we're rough, tough and in top physical shape as you can imagine being on a course such as this one.

As far as the course goes, it's in good control and the worst is over. Last Monday we went over the obstacle course. I sent a few pictures of it to you and it certainly was quite an experience. Climbed up and down mountain sides, cliffs, up ropes, and down, over water by swinging ropes, through streams up to our necks in mud, water and ice, jumping out of the top windows of houses into mud holes (neck and waist height), climbing rope ladders, through tunnels and then through the crawl trench under live fire. This was the pay off. I thought I'd never get through it! The water was muddy and ice cold and had deep holes here and there. We were numb by the time we finished it (200 yds long). It may sound a bit gruesome, but it was fun (in spots) but more particularly when we talked it over after it was all done. I was lucky with no after effects except my legs being a bit frost-bitten. They're ok. now. Practically everyone had that trouble.

We are into company tactics now. Yesterday I was platoon commander, so I was a busy boy in charge of flanking movements and then village clearing. There's more brains needed for success in the infantry than civilians realize. The private is no slouch if he's a good one and knows his work. There's no end to the learning in battle procedure. I did as well as anyone else including the officers when they were platoon commanders for the day, so I'm almost satisfied with my effort.

I just stopped off for dinner. The meals are on the whole very bad, but they don't starve us—lots of potatoes and vegetables but the meat is terrible—very little of it and poor stuff. There's usually a good supply of jam on the table so if there is a saturation of onion in the meal—there's the faithful and reliable jam.

Yesterday, we had the afternoon off so I prepared some lectures for next week and then went into Vernon, saw a show and had a good dinner. I went to a dance with a couple of other sergeants but never had one dance. The music was terrible and there was no one there that I could be bothered conversing with, so it was a dull time. Took away the monotony of Battle and Commando work anyway.

Yes, Mom, I'll certainly be glad to get back to Ipperwash where I can get nice quiet week ends at home after this course is over. I should be home about the middle of February unless I'm asked to remain as instructor or to play hockey—but that's very improbable. I wouldn't want to be stationed here any longer than was necessary. It's beautiful country but only to look at, but altogether too many mountains to climb.

Did I tell you there were men on this course in my platoon from Jamaica, Bermuda, San Francisco and Miami. They came from all over our continent so sometimes we get into some great talking sessions. It's an eduction in itself.

Some of the boys stroke off the days till the end of the course. The time is going fast though and the course is getting more interesting as it does, so it won't be l telling you all my experiences and abou Provinces and the train ride through the Rockies.

Have our final exam on Tuesday so guess I'd better study up a bit. Look after yourselves and it won't be long now.

Love,

Tuesday, Feb. 1/44

Dear Mother and Dad,

I'm two days late in writing this week. I can just imagine what you are saying when Dad comes in saying "no mail from Bob"! However, I'm still in there pitching and with the last days of the course gradually being finished.

The course finishes Saturday, Feb 5, and I expect to be on the train that night and heading East once more. I'm hoping that they will give me a few days off after I finish and get back to camp and then I'll be able to get home—and rest and visit. Boy, will I enjoy it too.

I was hoping to be able to get out to Vancouver, but the "bums" back at Ipperwash won't give us the few days to go there from here. A couple of the other boys out here from Ipperwash tried to get leave for that purpose and were refused. "This is the Army"! Makes you mad sometimes at their bull headedness.

This last week is a tough one. We're doing schemes in the mountains all day and even though we've been chasing those mountain goats for four weeks now, we still find it's hard on the condition.

Saturday night another Sergeant and I went down to Kelowna by bus for a change and to see the country. Went to a dance and met some new people—but mainly the good part about the trip was that we forgot about Vernon Battle School for awhile. The road is terrific ma. It winds up around the mountains and the lake. No guard rail and plenty of sharp turns. You wouldn't enjoy the trip, but it was really a great sight as we travelled along.

Have been playing a little hockey and it has been wonderful to get those old skates on again and chase a puck around. Played last night and won in overtime. Good game.

Wednesday night we have a scheme called night attack, Thursday morning we have dawn attack so it promises to be very interesting and also very invigorating!

Thanks a lot for your letter, pop. It's nice to get one from you once in a while.

Continuing on—I got the bracelet to-day safe and sound and it's swell mother! I like the big chain—just the type I like and thanks again. That will have to do for presents for some time now. I've been thinking that I should have my initials put on my ring, because when we get overseas we can't have any identification tags or rings which would tell the intelligence what unit you belong to. The same applies to my identification bracelet so unless I can get a "Canadian Infantry Corps Insignia" I don't think I'll have anything else put on it. I'm delighted with it, ma, so thanks again.

Bye for now -

Wed. Feb. 16/44
Ipperwash

Dear Mother and Dad,

Just a note to let you know your sonny is back at Ipperwash safe and sound and working hard already. I'm Orderly Sergeant to-day so I've a couple of minutes to spare—thus the letter. I'm a corporal once more—there's no opening at present for a sergeant. It's not pleasant to have to get back to the two stripes but it all takes time—more than I've taken as yet, it seems.

It was grand being home, ma. I think you could see how much I enjoyed being there with you two. Thanks for everything, particularly the washing job which was a big one—also the meals which were delightful—every one a treat. I'd better learn to wash sometime. I made a fair job of some of it in Vernon, but need a little more practice.

I'm still in #3 Company, so address will be the same. The ex- Mountie is still here with same rank as myself. In our new bunch of men we have Syl Apps, the noted hockey player. He's in my platoon—and gets the dickens same as the rest—from me. No favourites. Haven't had much work with him as yet. Rather quiet and a good man. Big fellow!

This will be all for the present.

Love from youngest

In Europe, planning for "Overlord" was going ahead and the Canadian Army of course was involved. As early as February the combined Chiefs of Staff had decided to divert some Canadian divisions from Italy to Northwest Europe. On March 8th General Stuart toured the Army camps with Montgomery and said that he had never seen such a splendid body of men and that he was most impressed with the high quality of the Canadian soldier.

Back in Canada, Bob was posted to an Army base near Sussex, New Brunswick. There was still no word of him being posted overseas and he was an instructor for demonstration platoons. The demonstration platoons consisted of the very best soldiers who were rigorously trained to do all the battle drills with absolutely perfect timing and no mistakes. They were used to "demonstrate" to the other soldiers exactly how a maneuver should be done. The battle drill would include climbing 10 foot walls, going hand over hand on ropes, running with heavy packs, going over barbed wire, all the things Bob had learned at Vernon and which are essential to infantry soldiers in actual battle situations.

Wed. Mar. 22/44

Dear Mother and Dad,

Hope this letter will reach you in time for Friday the 24th - your wedding anniversary. I'm right on the date, aren't I—It's your 34th isn't it? It seems like a long time, but I'll bet you two don't think it's been so long since you started up housekeeping together. I wished we all could be together for celebrating days like these, but now we must blame it on the Army, Air Force and Navy. Little did you probably ever think that you would be blam-

ing them for keeping your sons away from your anniversaries, but since there are other homes the same way, we can't do much except hope that it's over soon and living can come back to normal.

Marriage is the big step in life and I know it. I've said it before and I'll say it again, if I'm half as fortunate as you pop, I'll be happy and while I'm at it, ma, I think you were on your toes, too, about 34 years ago!

I don't know whether it's my inferiority complex or not, but it's going to take a lot of nerve on my part to ever ask someone to go through life with me—even when I do get in a position to be in a marrying mood. However, it's the least of my worries now!

Anyway, mes parents, congratulations on your wedding anniversary and hope I'm home for your next one.

My work here sure has started with a bang! I've worked every night this week so far and it looks like it will continue for some time. I'm helping to train men for demonstrations as well as doing some platoon commanding demonstrations myself. The demo. platoon isn't ready to put on the drills themselves so that's extra work for me. I do this along with my regular instructional duties so I'm a busy boy. I'm getting a great experience here and should mean a lot when it's entered on my documents. Am glad it's only temporary, for it is a big responsibility and hard work as well as too plentiful also.

Life here is same as I told you before. Nothing but army work. If we get through work in time I slip down the Y.M.C.A. hut or Salvation Army hut in the camp and see a show. Can usually see a new one every night, but that gets rather tiresome before long.

To-morrow is a big day with five demonstrations on the syllabus, so I'd better look up my notes and have a good sleep. It's 9 p.m. (8 your time) anyway so adios for now. Best of everything for the 24th to you, my mom and pop, whom I've always respected, admired as examples, and loved as a son should. No one can take the places of your mother and father and having you two is plenty to be thankful for. I don't say it very often, but you know it's always there. You've done so much for me, I wish I could do something for you—but there'll come a day.

Love to you both

Mon. March 24/44

Dear Mother and Dad,

I'm a day late, but I hope you don't mind too much. First of all, ma, thanks once more for those cookies and that sandwich spread.

Saturday I went to Moncton again for the week end. There's really nothing to do there, but when you can scrounge a week end, the change is wonderful for you, as you can imagine, and it's the best place to go to around here with the short week ends we get. There was a big Victory Loan parade there on Sunday. Lots of airmen, sailors and soldiers, but boy were they ever sloppy marchers.

Things are still buzzing here in usual busy manner although there are many rumours as to when this course will fold up. It is possible that it may end in two or three weeks unless more officers arrive. The sooner the better is all I can say. I wouldn't have minded the place too much, if I had gotten a decent deal here about a promotion, however, I consider myself as good as the rest and as a matter of fact I know more about battle drill than a good many others and I know the man in charge of the training knows it. There had to be an experienced corporal to be in the demonstration platoon's hut and mother them, so I guess I was "Joe'd" being the only corporal. I'm getting good experience, however, so I can't kick on that score.

My old company commander from Ipperwash is here now as an instructor. He was at Vernon while I was and I know him and like him very much. Talked to him to-day and he wondered why I hadn't been given that third stripe. Told him I'd been "Joe'd" as the saying goes and he said he'd see what he could do for me. He suggested this himself so you can see what sort of a man he is. Would be my luck to be made a sergeant just when the training is over, then I return to Ipperwash and probably take it over again. I'm very much disgusted with the set up. Some of the sergeants and officers that are parading around here make me good and mad. The sergeant major has done his best for me (I think) and they all think it's a gyp, but nothing seems to come to me but promises.

Enough of that stuff now. I really don't mind battle drill, although it is a bit tiresome at times.

Love

Sunday, Apr. 30/44

Dear Mom and Dad,

Sunday again! The time goes very fast when you are busy and last week sure flew. Yesterday we had Victory Loan parade here and the officers still here marched along with the demonstration platoon from A-34. with me at the head of the platoon. Wow! Was I a sensation when I tripped over my own feet (of course I didn't, but I wondered what it would be like if I did).

We are through demonstrating and instructing the officers here now and it's hard to say what will happen next week. A lot can, but I'll let you know just as soon as I can. There's a new rumour every day. Latest is that we'll be here for another two months instructing student officers before they go to Brockville.

My old Company Commander, Captain McCloud, went to the Colonel about me, and I saw the letter he gave him. It was quite flattering so my old Captain friend has done his best for me. My C.S.M. (Company Sergeant Major) told me the results, that possibly I would be made a sergeant in the near future and a few other promises, which I'll tell you if they ever materialize. I'm not getting excited. I've learned to accept things in the army only if you have them right in the palm of your hand. But that doesn't mean I don't work for them. So, nothing but promises yet!

Yesterday and to-day were really beautiful days and I enjoyed playing war in such weather. This morning we were all out for church parade and it left a good feeling in me about everything. I was glad we had to get up for it or I would have missed that good fresh morning. It was really a perfect morning.

Love and Kisses -

Wed. May 10/44
Montreal

Dear Mom and Dad,

Sorry I didn't write Sunday as I usually do, but I've been tripping around and time for writing has been at a minimum. I came here to Montreal yesterday and am having a lovely visit.

Last Friday they told us (the instructors) at Sussex that we wouldn't be needed for 10 days so I immediately hopped the train for Montreal. I had enough money for that. I've been looking around the city and have been having a swell time. Too bad I didn't get home but since this is extra time off, I thought I'd like to see Montreal thoroughly when I had the chance.

All the officers have left now. We have to hang around to train some C.O.T.C. instructors before their men come in to Sussex. It will last about three weeks then I should be through here and back to Ipperwash again for awhile. I'll get my furlough as soon as I can after that while the getting is good.

It sure is wonderful to get away like this for a change and have a bit of fun. Sussex is a dull place to stay in for very long and I've been having a quiet time of it there.

Hope you two are ok. Thinking of the lake no doubt now. I hope I can be up there this summer for awhile.

Well, it's about all for now. Be seeing you soon, I expect. Be good. I'll tell you the rest of my escapades later.

Love

In this next letter (May 22) Bob mentioned a box from his mother. Most mothers of servicemen regularly sent boxes to their sons—with their favourite food, some needed articles of clothing and little luxuries. This became even more important when the son was in Europe. Also, in most towns, the church groups sent boxes to the boys in their parish. These boxes and the letters from home were great morale builders for the servicemen.

Mon. May 22/44

Dear Mother and Dad,

Yesterday I didn't get around to writing you. These C.O.T.C. cadets arrived and that meant a lot of extra work. Then at night I saw a show put on by a U.S.O. travelling troupe so my time was pretty occupied.

Your box arrived to-day, ma, and everything weathered the trip very well.

I've got back into the swing of the army life again and find things a bit dull but I'm bearing up. I hope I make Ontario and Ipperwash by the end of June anyway. I've been out here long enough. My tour of duty ends then, so it had better be back to the old camp.

How I love thoughts of those summer days at Inverhuron. Hope I get a chance to ride the waves in my canoe this summer. What sport! I'm still a kid!

I was taken for a coloured boy in a picture the other day, so I guess my summer tan is returning again—sort of a hardened mahogany.

Not much news, as you see. Nothing happens here but eating, sleeping and working!

Love from your youngest

Thurs. May 25/44

Dear Mom and Dad,

Glad to get your letter, ma, as usual. I look forward to your "news weekly" and you're doing a good job. Your letters usually arrive on Wednesdays when they're written Sundays so it takes a little while for them to travel out here.

The C.O.T.C. cadets are here now and my job is helping train the demo platoon and put on demonstrations as I did for the British officers. The work is quite a bit different, with not so much battle drill. We've been busy training the men in new demonstrations for the new course.

It's a good thing I'm tired these days and satisfied with bed early, since I'm waiting very impatiently for pay-day. I think I'll manage till Wednesday though. I'm just getting over that Montreal holiday. It was worth it, but it's rather an expensive city. When next pay-day comes, all will be fine again.

I'll sure be glad when I get through here and back to Ontario and see you two again. Been quite awhile now. I'm fed up with this set up. I work hard and never get anywhere and the demo platoon is darn near sending me nuts sometimes. I'm hut corporal for 60 men and that's a job when they're a bunch of irresponsible kids!

However, I get over my grouchy moments with them somehow or other. I think I'll be a crank or a crab by the time I leave here. You wouldn't know me when I work I'm sure.

Lots of love -

The Army never did give Bob a chance at officer's training although he usually was given officer's work to do. Perhaps it was because he hadn't been attached to any specific regiment, and moving around the country as he did, he continually had new officers who didn't know him and his capacity for leadership. Also moving about so much never allowed him to feel attached to any unit and make good friends.

Sun. May 28/44

Dear Mom and Dad,

I've had a nice easy day—up for breakfast and took the boys over to church parade. This afternoon I caught up on some washing so that now I can be clean for a few days more. You should have seen me this afternoon bending over that tub scrubbing my shirts, socks, and underwear, etc. We've had a lot of hot weather lately, and this washing chore has been happening just a little too frequently.

Our writing room is filled at present with a lot of C.O.T.C. boys sending letters home with their first impressions of this army game.

Yesterday there was a bit of excitement around camp. A mortar bomb acted up on some of the men and a bit of tough luck ensued with six or eight on the injured list. I believe they're coming along ok. though. Very rarely happens, but some things can't be helped.

I went to a dance last night at Sussex. It was such a nice night out I had to do something. It was nothing wonderful, but I had a fairly good time and forgot about the army for awhile.

We're busy demonstrating and instructing these days. Most of the work is on the section level and doesn't go as far as even platoon shows, so it's only elementary battle drill that these cadets are getting. The work is getting dull and monotonous, but I have the satisfaction of knowing that the big boys think I'm doing a good job. Of course, for my own ego, I like to think I can do this work better than anyone else in camp and I'm pretty darn sure I do too! Patting yourself on the back makes you feel better sometimes! The reason I haven't got my promotion is because my work in the hut and outside should be done by a corporal and they have no one to take my place. I hardly think it's fair but there's the story. They didn't tell me that but I know. I get plenty disgusted sometimes. If I had remained at Ipperwash I would have been a sergeant by now. However, take things as they come, and never count on anything till it happens.

'Bout all for now bosses. I hope you get to the lake and enjoy some of this nice weather. I'm enjoying it.

So long for now

Love from your youngest

Although not mentioned in Bob's letters, the big war news in June was the Allied invasion of Europe, the offensive called "Overlord" which took place on June 6. The choice of Normandy for the landings was a surprise for the German Army and the story of the success of "D" day is well known. The Canadian Army 3rd Division played an important role, with some 14,000 soldiers involved but almost one thousand of these became casualties (335 killed).

The Canadians stormed the beach between Bayeux and the River Orne (see Map 1). They occupied a position in the centre of the British front. There had been a massive aerial bombardment first, followed by a naval bombardment. The plan was for the Canadians to get 10 miles inland by nightfall, but this was not obtained. The enemy fortifications and the resistance, under Field Marshalls Rommel and von Rundstedt, were more formidable than had been expected.

However, by June 15, as many as 500,000 Allied troops were ashore in France and the construction of two artificial harbours was underway. Harbours were the big problem, since such a huge army required a great deal of supplies and equipment. The capture of the German-held Channel ports was to be a task given to the Canadian Army.

Sunday June 11/44

Dear Pop,

Of course, this letter is also for mother, but since I just

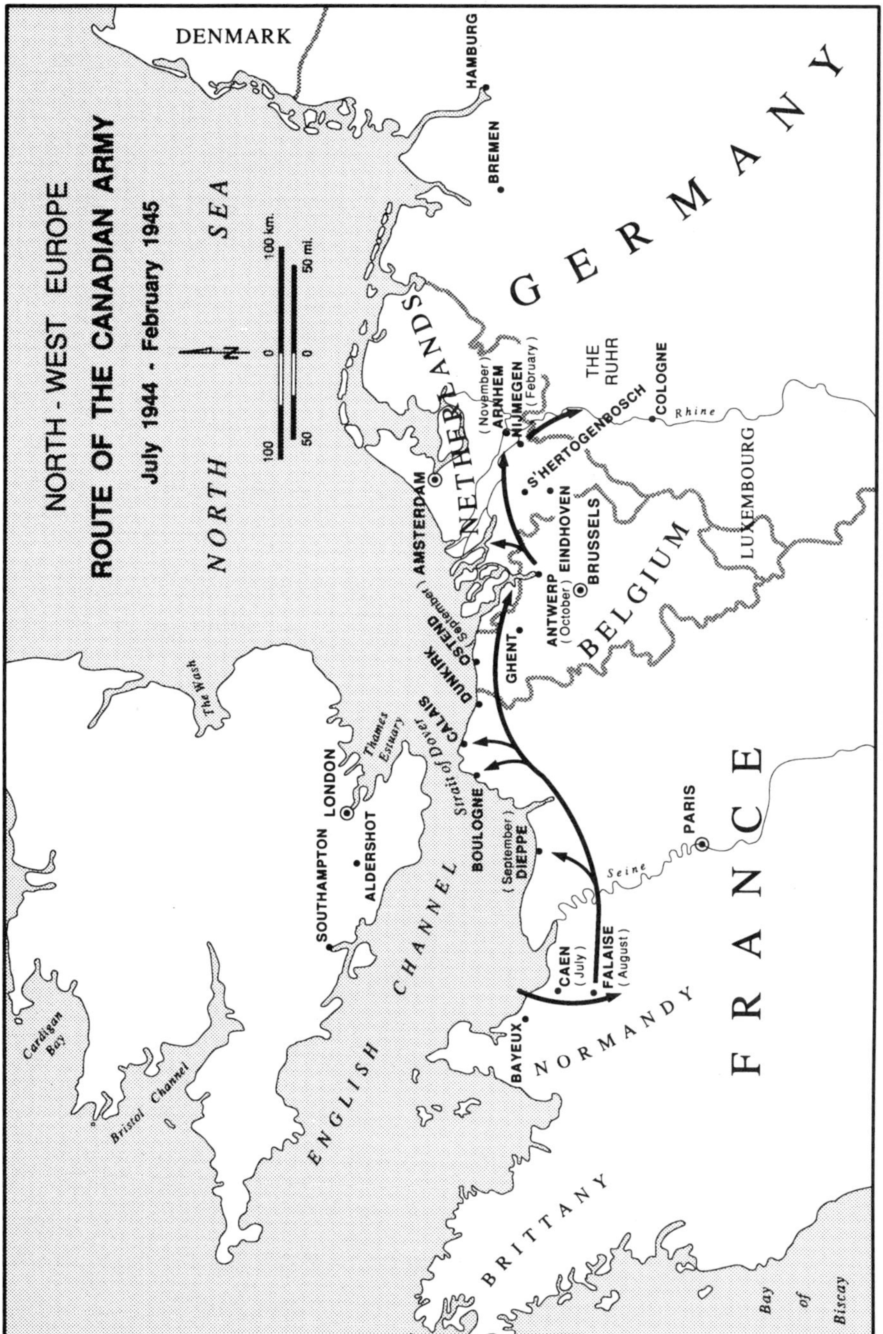
NORTH - WEST EUROPE
ROUTE OF THE CANADIAN ARMY
July 1944 - February 1945
NORTH SEA
100 km.
50 ml.
DENMARK
HAMBURG
BREMEN
GERMANY
NETHERLANDS
AMSTERDAM
(November) ARNHEM
NIJMEGEN (February)
S'HERTOGENBOSCH
EINDHOVEN
THE RUHR
COLOGNE
Rhine
LUXEMBOURG
BELGIUM
BRUSSELS
ANTWERP (October)
GHENT
OSTEND (September)
DUNKIRK
CALAIS
BOULOGNE
(September) DIEPPE
Strait of Dover
The Wash
Thames Estuary
LONDON
ALDERSHOT
SOUTHAMPTON
Cardigan Bay
Bristol Channel
ENGLISH CHANNEL
PARIS
Seine
CAEN (July)
FALAISE (August)
BAYEUX
NORMANDY
BRITTANY
FRANCE
Bay of Biscay

Map 1

found out that to-day is "Father's Day" I'll address it to you. Sorry I didn't know sooner about this being your day, dad, but I'm thinking of you to-day. I should have at least had a letter there for you. Mother says your heel has been bothering you; I hope you've conquered that by now. Won't be long now till you'll be bowling, swimming(?) and playing horse shoes down at good old Inverhuron. It sure is the place! I was sure a lucky boy to have had so much when I was home. I guess I was spoiled for I don't think I appreciated it as much as I should have. 'Course, that's the usual case with everyone—never satisfied!

Monday, I expect to know for sure whether I get my furlough this Thursday or not so may hold this letter over till I do know. If I do get it I'll be in Chesley Saturday, I hope.

Nothing exciting has been happening here lately. One of the chaps who got hit with the mortar bomb died last week. Some are still in the hospital so that was a sad affair. Other than that I guess all the news is coming from France and Italy. There'll be many anxious people. Got a letter from Fred and he's on a course at present so will not be in the invasion for the time being. I wish Fred [Fred Stokes was his best friend from Chesley. He was the minister's son who lived next door. They had been counsellors together at camp on Lake Temagami] *and I could have been together in this. I miss a pal like him. Most of the sergeants here are married and the ones that aren't never will be I don't imagine. Anyway, with the set up in the Army, it's impossible to have a pal for long—one of you will be moved and you're alone again.*

Well pop, I should say something flowery about you to-day, but you know how I feel about everything and that you're the tops *of all pops. Wish I could send you a $1,000 cheque but my pay was just a small mid-month advance this time. Maybe the next one at the end of the month, I can give the down payment.*

Love

Mon. July 10/44

Dear Mother and Dad,

Well, I'm down to earth once more after a perfect holiday [spent in his favourite place, Inverhuron]. *By the way, the earth is muddy and dirty too; it was raining when I arrived here last night and it's still a bit drizzly. The weather has been good here lately, so I'm hoping it'll change—but not too much on the hot side.*

First of all, thanks to you two for everything which sure includes a lot. Being home and seeing you again sure was wonderful in itself and being down at that best place of all, at the cottage, was a morale builder. I never enjoyed a holiday so much.

The train ride to Montreal was fast and not too bad but the rest from there on was a nightmare. I was lucky enough to meet Sergeants Smith and Rowe in Montreal, so I had company the rest of the way. I always meet someone in Montreal I know—this time it was a kid by the name of Bagshaw now in the Navy that I knew at Western. Used to stay at Huron, so we had quite a conflab. Jim knows him too.

To-night, I had two more needles so my left arm is a bit stiff. It was still noticeable that I was positive to that test I had before I left, so it was ok that I didn't bother Dr. Dawson. Rest your mind, ma?

Hope you are having a good time at the lake. It certainly was hard to leave there when everything was so perfect.

All for now - Love -

The 2nd Canadian Division, the one to which Bob was eventually attached, arrived in Normandy during the first week in July. By July 9th the Canadians had occupied Caen and the battle had been hard and bloody. They were faced with several of Hitler's best panzer divisions, which had been brought south from the Calais area when Hitler decided that there wouldn't be any sea borne attack in that area. Hitler had also replaced Rundstedt with General Kluge in early July, after Rundstedt had been fired for advising Hitler to make peace with the Allies. There were a good many Canadian casualties and the need for replacements was becoming acute.

Sunday July 16/44

Dear Mother and Dad,

I got paid on Saturday so I decided to go to the sea for the week end. I went to Moncton and called up some C.O.T.C. boys who had taken their summer training from me and they invited me to a party with them Saturday night. Had a swell time and to-day we went to St. du Chene on the ocean shores and I had my first afternoon of swimming in salty water. It's just as everyone tells you, salty and very buoyant. It was a swell change.

Sure wish I could drop down to Inverhuron for a week-end and see you all and my canoe. I was spoiled, with such a grand furlough to remember. I thanked you before, but thanks again.

Not much excitement here this week except for a fire which took three of our huts and that wasn't good. The whole camp is just a fire trap and fires are plentiful here.

How's pop's bowling and have you tried the fishing at the point yet?

Love from youngest -

In Europe, the Canadian army was seeing action in Normandy. On July 18th, the 2nd and 3rd Canadian Infantry Divisions took part in an operation called "Atlantic" in the area south and east of Caen. The area was mostly wheat fields, which offered little protection to the tanks or infantry. In this area the Essex Scottish regiment, to which Bob was eventually attached, was struck by enemy tanks and literally cut to pieces. The Germans had assembled six armoured divisions in the area, including the 116th Panzer Division, which Bob would eventually meet up with in Germany. Meanwhile, Bob was still instructing at Sussex.

Wed. July 26/44

Dear Mother and Dad,

I'm sorry that I'm a little late this week in my correspondence, but I thumbed to the ocean side again last week end and therefore my usual Sunday letter had to be suspended until now.

I had another nice time at this summer resort again. It is quite a way to go, but, the change is wonderful and although the place is nothing like Inverhuron it's the best under the circumstances. I'm lucky for that much. Guess Jeff would give anything for a week end like that. The sergeant I was with was good company and the two of us lay on the beach and got as much out of the holiday as possible.

Before I say any more, I do believe that the 26th of July is pop's big day. I'm sorry this letter is slow in getting to you, pop, but I'm thinking of you and hope you have a swell day.

The new men started their course Tuesday and don't get their battle work for a few weeks. Maybe I'll be getting out of here soon 'cause they don't give much battle drill to these men before they go over. Most of them are armoured corps, or signal corps, so they don't need it like infantry men. Yesterday a Captain left for another camp. He's been here since March and before he left he told me he'd recommended me and that he hoped action would come soon. It's getting monotonous now! He'd been in Africa and Italy and had the Military Cross so he'd been around. He was the sort of officer that men would follow well—what we call a "square shooter". I never knew him very well but was sorry to see him leave.

Love to all -

Thurs. Aug. 5/44

Dear Mother and Dad,

Late again! Last week end I was at St. John and had a swell get to-gether with brother Art [who was now a lieutenant in the Navy]. *He phoned me on Thursday so we met at the Navy League Club. It was rather humiliating to stay at such a place, however, I must say that it was certainly better than the Salvation Army Hostel that I stayed at the last time I visited St. John. It was really a very nice place and I found the sailor boys looked very nice too in their "sailor suits"!*

Art looks very smart in his outfit. We did very little at St. John but had the visit together which was better than anything else that could have been thrown in for any week end. Art will probably know by this Saturday what will happen to him as far as the Navy job is concerned. I hope all turns out well.

I met a couple of old Western boys now in the Navy so it was like old times and a regular reunion. Art seemed to know practically the whole Navy that was visiting in St. John last week end.

My demonstration platoon left today on draft, so I'll be doing new interesting things now; I don't know just what it'll be as yet. I'm hoping to leave here soon. My job here is done since battle drill is practically nil on the new course we're on now, but M.D.7 (Military District) hasn't released us yet. There are two brothers here who are very poor specimens as officers that are a bit hard to get along with, and it appears as if they hate to see anyone improve their status in the army, so I can't expect anything from them. I'm hoping that I can get back to Ipperwash soon and have a show-down.

Like the rest of your boys, I miss Inverhuron and everyone. The war seems to be rolling along in good style so maybe we can be a bit optimistic and hope it'll be over soon.

Love from son -

Since "D" day the war news had been good. The Allied forces, including the Canadians, had driven successfully through Normandy and had captured Caen.

However, already in August, the Canadian Army was known to be short of infantry troops because of the heavy casualties. General Stuart had alerted Ottawa that there was *"a shortage of about 3,000 general duty infantry personnel"* and he urged that the NRMA men be sent overseas and the Minister of Defence, Ralston agreed. However, Prime Minister Mackenzie King did not agree.

There had been a counter offensive by the Germans in August—an attempt to break through the Allied troops to the sea. It was not successful and many thousands of German prisoners were taken in the very bloody fighting of the Falaise Gap. The Germans had suffered the greatest disaster in modern military history. The bodies of German soldiers littered the ground along with some 8,000 dead horses. Pete Heaton of the Essex Scottish Regiment, who was injured during this operation, has told me that the sounds of dying horses is almost human and very upsetting.

The Canadians were ordered by Montgomery to completely destroy the enemy in Northwest France and to push rapidly to the Seine River. The Germans managed to pull back across the Seine the greater part of troops that had survived the Falaise Gap. By the end of August the Battle of Normandy was over, and the Allies had a great victory, and on August 25th, Paris had been liberated. The enemy had lost 400,000 men killed, wounded or captured (200,000 prisoners of war). But the Canadian casualties were not insignificant. For August alone there were 9,000, of whom 2,200 were killed. As always, it was the infantry who suffered the most.

Sept. 9/44
Ipperwash Camp (again)

Dear Mother and Dad,

With such a lovely pen to write with I should be a better writer now both in legibility and frequency! Thanks for everything ma and you too pop. My leave at home had everything I wanted and then some. Coming away is the part that isn't so good but there have been many others who have gone through it before me. We have our little job to do and that's about all that can be said. It can't be long before it's over now though. I wont be like those poor fellows who've been over there since this thing began.

I'm still here at Ipperwash and already I'm looking forward to being home again but I am also glad that I'm going to have my chance too [Bob was referring here to the rumour that he would soon be sent overseas]*—officer or not. That part doesn't* *bother me anymore!*

I have no idea how long I'll be here nor do I know my future address, but I'm almost certain the next stop will be Debert N.S. where we will be kept (and trained at the same time) for a while.

Yesterday my corporal friend Bartholomew and I managed to get into London for the day. He had to get a pair of glasses. Had a nice time and saw a lot of my old friends as well as a good show. Was a nice change and glad to have had the visit there.

To-day we have been very busy at draft work. Had my medical this afternoon and all was ok.

Well, parents, be good and look after yourselves. Take it as easy as possible and please don't worry about me. I'll write my letters and let you know all about my free travels with the Army.

Love

In Europe, Hitler determined to delay the Allies the use of the Channel ports as long as possible, since bringing supplies from the French ports was causing strain on the Allies communications. To meet this crisis, Hitler recalled von Rundstedt, the most able of his generals.

Wed. Sept. 13/44

Dear Mom and Dad,

I'm just scrawling a hurried note just before we leave this afternoon. I believe it's Debert, N.S. but I, of course, am not certain.

Glad to get your letter and also the parcel. It was a tough job packing up. I am to remain a Corporal until I get overseas. I have a platoon of my own and they're a good bunch of men—no officer as yet. This'll likely be until Debert anyway.

Well, pop, be good and look after yourself; — you too ma.

I'll write as often as possible

Love,

Meanwhile, in the war zone in Europe, Eisenhower and Montgomery realized in September that it was essential for the Allies to maintain the momentum of the campaign, and to destroy the enemy, if possible, before he could recover from the defeat in Normandy.

The 2nd Canadian Division reached Dieppe on Sept 1st - to find the Germans gone and the population jubilant at their liberation. Dieppe also afforded the Allies a much needed port closer to the British supply centres. By September 3, the British had captured Brussels and the next day had entered Antwerp. The Second Canadian Army had entered Holland on September 12th, in the area south of Eindhoven (Map 1). Obtaining the use of the major port of Antwerp was essential to the Allied cause, but it couldn't be used in September because the Germans controlled the Scheldt Estuary between Antwerp and the sea (some 50 miles). Actually, the first convoy entered Antwerp harbour only on November 28th. The port at Ostend was captured on September 9th and was open to traffic by September 26th.

Back in Canada, there was a bitter controversy over conscription. On September 19th, the ***Globe and Mail*** published a story by Conn Smythe (of subsequent hockey fame) who had been invalided home from the war. He made the accusation that the Canadian Army was being bled to death on the European battlefields because of lack of replacements. This story was to have major implications for the government before the year was ended.

Sat. Sept. 16/44

Dear Mother and Dad,

It's Debert, N.S. where I am now, and it's quite a spot. We got here early last night taking about two days for the trip. We had company from other camps as we went along and ended up with quite a bunch. It's a camp much like Borden and it's quite easy to lose yourself in it—I hardly know where I am but I do know that Truro is 10 miles away and quite a few of us are going into the town and look it over to-night.

The trip was very good considering it was such a long one and with so much company with us.

Next week we'll start into special training and it promises to be very interesting work, more along the lines I like and into the battle drill that I instructed in. We are still corporals here but in name only—(not pay which is bad), and we're hoping something can be done about it. I have to keep on with the instructing here as well as take the training myself. There is rumour that some men may be kept as instructors but I think I can get out of that. I've served my sentence at that and I'm with a good bunch of boys right now and I'd like to stay with them. Besides, there's no future in that and I need a change. [It was obvious from this comment that Bob was tiring of the perpetual training and instructing, and was eager to be sent to Europe—where the action was].

I've met many old boys here that I've met at Vernon and Sussex, etc. I keep meeting them everywhere and it's great talking over old times. Most of my demo platoon from Sussex are here now too.

I've still got my cake and peanut butter. Think I'll save it for awhile till I get posted somewhere else. When that will be no one knows but there are plenty of rumours as usual. I hope it's soon so I can practise what I've preached about for so long.

Look after yourselves and be good. Don't let any of those students push you around, pop!!!!!

Love from the N.S. kid
(at present)

There was controversy between Eisenhower and Montgomery about how to proceed against Germany. General Montgomery wished to invade Germany through the lower Rhine delivering a "knockout" blow on the Ruhr while Eisenhower preferred a more broadly based attack. However, Montgomery won approval for operation "Market Garden" to begin September 17th. The plan was to have U.S. Airborne divisions dropped near Eindhoven and Grave, and British paratroopers near Arnhem (see Map 1). The British captured Nijmegen and its bridge intact, but Arnhem was a failure since the German resistance and counter attack was much more successful than had been anticipated. The Arnhem story is famous and the subject of the movie ***"A Bridge Too Far".*** Some 10,000 British Airborne troops were landed, in gliders or by parachute, in the area near Nijmegen and Arnhem and attempted to attain the northern side of the river, and secure the bridge at Arnhem. They were surrounded by German troops and managed to survive for about a week, then had to withdraw. They suffered terrible casualties: 1,200 officers and men were killed and only 2,160 returned to their regiments. Montgomery was not to attain his vision of a dagger attack on Germany's heart-land that autumn. After Arnhem, it was apparent to the Allies that the war would not be ended in 1944, as had been hoped.

Meanwhile, the Canadians attacked and took the port of Boulogne, capturing more than 9,000 German prisoners, and then advanced further along the coast to attack Calais. In Canada, Bob knew that he would soon be going overseas.

Debert, N.S.
Fri. Sept. 22/44

Dear Mother and Dad,

Debert Camp is quite a spot. The training so far is not so tough but some are finding it otherwise. I'm lucky to have had the training I've had because I'm ahead of the rest when it comes to the work we're at now. The instructors (sergeants) can ask me about different things which makes me laugh!

We've been here a week to-night and I find the time has gone very quickly. The weather has been very disagreeable here since we arrived—rain every day and the mosquitoes don't know that their season is over now. They're bad!

Truro is a very dull town but they sell good bacon and tomato sandwiches there, so we're satisfied with our visit if we devour one of them—or two.

I'm going to send my watch and my glasses home. My watch won't stand the pounding and has the small second hand off and my glasses have one unbroken lens out. Just get the two articles repaired for me and I'll pick them up personally in a little while after the chores are done. Won't have much need for the glasses now and they're awfully hard to look after. I should have them, but don't get much time to read or even see shows these days.

Look after yourselves and don't work too hard!

Love from your youngest

Mon. Oct. 2/44

Dear Mom and Dad,

I'm really sorry I haven't written sooner to thank you for that swell box of food that you and Dad sent. I had a busy day on my birthday. It was our work night and it was 2.30 that night before I found my bed.

<u>Tuesday</u>. I actually fell asleep while writing this last night. This afternoon we're having a break for a change. The Governor General and Princess Alice were here this morning for a big inspection. It's a terrible day—cold and rainy so I guess they fig-

ured we needed to be thawed out. They're a pretty smart looking pair, those two. I had a fine position as marker in my platoon so I got a good view of them and also in the march past.

Sunday I went in to Truro after I'd done a little washing and the other three N.C.O.s that I usually run around with, actually went to church with me. We almost had to force one past the door, but I think he enjoyed the service after all. The music was good - not as good as our choir in the old days—and it was nice to be in a real church for a change—a United Church too. I intended to write Sunday, but you see how the time went.

The time seems to go fast here, but with only army activities, so there's not a great deal of really personal news to give you. Some of the boys are finding the training hard but so far for me it has been ok. and nothing new. I do find myself quite tired at night though and go to bed rather early.

I've had a cold lately but other than that I'm in good fighting shape. Hope you two are looking after yourselves. Must be a bit quiet after a busy summer with all your visitors.

We're having (I suppose) the typical N.S. weather these days which makes it rather disagreeable but other than that, everything is rolling along smoothly. Only wish that now I've started on my way, that I'd get all the way, but I can't do any thing about that.

All for now
Love from son

There couldn't have been many infantry soldiers so well

trained as Bob. He had been in the army about a year and a half and was a graduate of many courses. His remark *"that I'd get all the way"* refers, of course to going overseas. After so many months of training he was eager to see real action. And it was to come quickly.

In Europe, Calais had been liberated on October 1 by Canadian units, including cousin Jeff's Cameron Highlanders. They captured 7,000 prisoners while suffering only 300 casualties. The battle to gain the area of South Beveland (the area between Antwerp and the sea) to open the port of Antwerp to Allied shipping was given to the Canadian 2nd Division and the fighting was very bitter with many casualties during the month of October. Actually the number of infantry casualties since the Normandy invasion had been very much underestimated by the High Command and the word had gone out to bring infantry reinforcements quickly to Europe. The next letter from Bob to his parents (October 8th) was his last from Canadian soil.

Sunday Oct. 8/44

Dear Mom and Dad,

Have just left our canteen theatre after seeing a show there and have time to write you before I hit the old bed.

Got your letter and glad to get your news and views. It was a very good letter too ma, and I can just see how much of your time must go in just writing the three of us, let alone keeping up your other correspondence. I still think you should get a stencil or even get a typewriter and try your hand at that.

Things here are the same as ever. Next week promises to be a busy one with a three day scheme and a few other special features. Promises to be very eventful with the weather as it is around here.

To-morrow is Thanksgiving Day. Sure wish I could be with you, but maybe next time it rolls around I'll help you devour that turkey.

By the way, have been thinking that since your boys are away and no one to do some of the chores like shovelling and ashes with winter coming in, I want you to take the money needed for that out of my roll in the bank every week. Get someone to do it—throwing in wood, etc. I owe you two money and you use it whenever you want. Just mark it down, and I'll get it eventually all paid up. Sure am thankful for my parents and I can do a few things for you even though I am away.

Won't be long till the football will be going again back in Ontario. Sure would like to see a few games this year. Last year I was at Long Branch and saw practically all the games while taking my courses there. Time has gone very fast since I joined the army 19 months ago now! Did I tell you I sport a big ribbon on my chest now—for the Battle of Canada, you know. It's the Canadian Volunteer Service Medal for 18 months of active service —<u>ACTIVE</u>. I at least have been active in seeing Canada—and doing Battle Drill as I have since January. I guess I couldn't have been much more active on this side of the Atlantic.

Bed time now, Love

Somewhere in England

In October, 1944, Ralston had told Mackenzie King of the desperate need for replacements in the Canadian Army, especially in the infantry. There were in October some 130,000 soldiers in the Army still in Canada while 15,000 replacements were urgently needed in Europe, but Mackenzie King did not want to impose conscription. It was well known that too many men were trained for the armoured and artillery corps and too few by far for the infantry. Certainly the new recruits didn't wish to volunteer for the infantry when it became known that the average life of a soldier in the front lines until he was killed, injured or captured was about four weeks.

As a result of the disagreement between Ralston and the Prime Minister, King accepted Ralston's resignation and appointed McNaughton as Minister of Defence on November 1st. McNaughton's appeal for NMRA personnel to "go active" failed, and on November 23rd the government passed an order in Council authorizing sending 16,000 of the NMRA men overseas. Many of these deserted, but before the war was over some 13,000 did go overseas. The first group left Halifax on January 3, 1945.

It is not clear why Bob had been 19 months in the Army—and still in Canada. It is certain that he was a well trained soldier. It is also true that he had leadership ability and was in excellent physical condition, so was of great use to the army in training new recruits in Canada.

The trip across the Atlantic was in the converted ***Mauritania*** with 6,000 troops aboard. They slept in hammocks, in three tiers, everywhere on the ship (even in the drained swimming pool). Meals went on continually with so many to feed, and a good many were seasick. Bob was a good sailor and never got seasick although the weather was very stormy and the ship changed course very frequently to avoid detection by enemy submarines.

The first day out of Halifax, he was "conscripted" along with others to help in the galley, peeling potatoes. The potato peelers were assigned to a passageway that crossed the ship from side to side. As the ship rolled to the port side, all the barrels of potatoes, men, and water would roll with it and crash into the side of the ship. Then the ship would begin rolling to starboard and the potato peelers would search frantically for something to hold onto, to prevent them sliding with the barrels of potatoes starboard. The officer in charge didn't perceive the problem until one poor soldier was hit by a barrel of potatoes and had his leg broken. However, the potato peeling had to continue, but from then on, in a passageway that ran lengthwise through the ship. Bob never cared much for peeling potatoes after that experience, and was glad when the coast of England was sighted.

The troop ship, ***Mauritania***, landed in Liverpool and the Canadian replacements were taken to the Canadian Army camp at Aldershot in Southern England. Bob hastened to write to his parents, since of course, he couldn't tell them in his earlier letters that he was en route to England. Like a good soldier, he was very careful about what he put in his letters from Europe, and none of them bore the mark of the censor.

Sunday, October 22/44

Somewhere in England

Dear Mother and Dad,

Greetings and salutations my dear parents! I have not been able to write you lately so I hope you have not been worried. Been rather busy as you no doubt surmised but things are back to normal and everything is under control.

You no doubt thought that I was a bit sick but you know nothing ever bothers me! I've tried out a few new things lately and have had a great time with my new experiences. I once tried sleeping in a hammock on my stomach (on board ship) but ma, that just doesn't work out.

I was going to send you a cablegram when I arrived in England but an ordinary letter I'm told gets to you practically as fast and I'm unable to get any airmail stamps to-night. Let me know how long it takes for you to receive this and we'll find out for certain. Will send an air mail later on and then we'll compare the two.

Lately I sent my watch to you. I hope it arrived safely. Was in a rush when I packed and sent it so I've been wondering about it. Dad can wear it till I come back and claim it. It isn't going but it shouldn't take much to have it repaired.

Fine weather here to-day but it's really cool and damp in the morning. I'm hoping to have a leave to go to London maybe next week-end, but I haven't been able to find out about it as yet.

Don't address any more letters to me as an N.C.O. for I have reverted to my confirmed rank as a private now and am known only as that.

I wouldn't mind if you could send me a few cigarettes now and then out of my account. It is a nasty habit I know, but I still like them once in awhile!! They are very cheap if sent to men overseas. The English cigarettes are terrible and expensive too.

My address here is #2 C.I.R.U. [Canadian Infantry Reserve Unit] *instead of #1. I don't know whether that parcel will ever reach me or not. Probably in six months or so.*

England is certainly quite a country. Very picturesque countryside and towns and cities everywhere. Had a grand trip through it and I had my eyes open all the time. The trains are peculiar with their small engines, tiny box cars and their odd "hoot hoots" but they certainly do a wonderful job. It's a wonderful system that they have. There are no railroad crossings at all.

Haven't seen any buzz bombs around yet and I guess it's a good thing.

This is about all for the present. It's getting rather late and I sure am tired to-night. I think I'm being the sort of son you expect of me and I'm having a swell time being that way too. I don't think it'll be long till we'll all be home and I can tell you all about England, and where I've been on my travels. I'm really sorry I didn't get over here sooner now that I am here, instead of serving that instructor's sentence and listening to promises, but now I suppose I am more prepared and the experience I had will help me a lot.

Right now I guess Dad's sitting in the choir at church and you are down in #7 pew, gazing up at him. Boy, what a Sunday when we're all there again!

Love from your "Blighter" son -

On October 18th, Montgomery and Eisenhower had met in Brussels to determine the next phase of the war. The job given to the Canadian army was to clear the Germans out of the area in the Netherlands south of the Maas River from 's Hertogenbosch westward and clear the area north of Beveland. In these low lying areas, some below sea level, the fighting was difficult and because of the flooded fields, the Allied tanks were useless.

In Aldershot in England, Bob wrote to his aunt and uncle of his experiences and the fact that he had once again been demoted to the rank of private.

Mon. Oct. 25/44

Dear Aunt Florence and Uncle Jim,

I just received a letter from you which you had written while at Chesley. It was forwarded on to me here in England. Got it in good time I'd say. Also heard from Mother too, so I was well looked after to-day.

I had a pleasant trip through a large part of England lately and I had my eyes wide open all the way (yes, just popping as you imagine). It certainly is a picturesque country with all the hedge rows and rock fences marking off the fields. I was sorry not to have seen Scotland, but maybe when I can get a leave, I can get up there.

I'm hoping to get a 36 hour leave this week-end, but things are too indefinite for leaves. Would likely go to London and maybe look up Uncle Jim's friend. London is in bounds for us once more, so I mustn't miss seeing that city if it's at all possible. I've been quite busy so I haven't even been out of the camp since my last trip. Hope to get a late pass (midnight) to-morrow and go to the nearest town.

The Nazi morons are still sending a few buzz-bombs over at nights. I heard one last night passing over probably heading for London. They sound like a stuttering tractor.

I'm still with my old N.C.O. pals, so I'm lucky there and am really finding everything ok. here. One of my pals broke his ankle at Debert, so we had to leave him there, however, he may catch up with us yet. There are lots of men here that I know. Some that I had in my platoons, but I think they have a bit of a liking towards me. Maybe because they don't have to do what I say now!! I'm back to my confirmed rank of private again.

Am hoping to get nearer Jeff soon. Maybe in a couple of weeks. That'll be all for now, folks. Look after yourselves. Was a blood donor to-day so I'm a bit tired.

Love and Kisses -

Somewhere in England
Tuesday, Oct. 31/44

Dear Mother and Dad,

Well, Pop, I hope you have been looking after Mother closely to-night (Hallowe'en). This is the night she usually gets the urge to prowl and scare the Chesley public.

Thursday I was told I could go to London on the week-end. Couldn't plan much, but Bartholomew and I went to the city and had a swell change seeing all we could. Tried to contact Uncle Jim's friend but was unable to. Saw Big Ben, Parliament Buildings, Nelson Monument, Piccadilly area, Trafalgar Square etc. and looked over a bit of blitzed London. There was an air-raid alert the night I was there and a couple of stray "doodle-bugs" went over. It's truly a great city, very old and historic as you know. Dad would have a wonderful time here, except he'd need a month to visit all the historical places. The underground railway system is really a wonderful feat and a great thing to see. I'm hoping to go on a tour next Sunday and see Buckingham Palace and Windsor Castle, etc. The King was out when I phoned him. Do hope he's in this time.

The weather has been amazingly fine the last few days. It's always quite damp and cool, and nights usually misty. Rains once practically every day for a few minutes anyway just to keep the record up, it seems.

While in London my eyes naturally looked at many of the fairer sex in England and ma, don't worry about me returning with a wife, if my first impressions continue. They're much more inter-

esting and more beautiful in Canada. Besides I can't understand what they're saying half the time.

Maybe if you can find an old time-ticker somewhere, ok. but not an expensive watch. A good watch if broken here might as well be thrown away. Just a few cigarettes that's all. Don't need and can't use anything else. Am well looked after here. Meals are naturally nothing like home, but I'm surviving and am not losing any weight. A few darn onions have gotten over here, so can't say as I like that part of it all. That weed grows every where!

Well, my dear bosses, this'll suffice for now. Everything's fine, I'm fine, and reports are fine so see that you two are fine. Don't work too hard and have fun.

Love from your youngest -

As a good son, Bob's special task in each letter was to assure his parents that he was fine and not too hateful of army life. He was getting closer to the continent where, by November 3rd, Belgium had been completely liberated, and the Canadian troops played an important role in the liberation. Throughout France and in Belgium, the people flocked to welcome the Allied troops and German soldiers were being taken prisoner in great numbers. From October 1 to November 8 some 41,000 were captured while the Allies suffered only 13,000 casualties, of whom 6,000 were Canadian.

In early November, the Canadian Army front ran from south of Nijmegen some 200 miles to Dunkirk. The main job of the Canadians for the next few weeks was to hold the ground they had, including the Nijmegen bridge. The Nijmegen area was of great importance to the Allies, especially the area north of the Waal River between Nijmegen and Arnhem, which was an Allied island in the midst of German-held territory. The infantry troops had to be extremely vigilant, and were constantly sent on patrols into enemy territory, under wretched conditions. The ground was generally flooded, and the weather was extremely cold. The winter of 1944 - 45 was to be one of the coldest winters on record in Western Europe.

Meanwhile Bob was in England but wouldn't remain there long. There was urgent need for infantry replacements on the continent.

Mon. Nov. 6/44

Dear Mother and Dad,

I hope you don't mind this writing being worse than usual, but I'm on my stomach in my bunk writing until the lights go out, and although I'm quite comfortable, it's not the best position for good results.

I've not had a letter from you directly from Chesley but Tuesdays have been my lucky days so far and I'm expecting some mail to-morrow. I've also found out that air-mail gets here in about five days, so that's much better than the ordinary mail run such as this letter, however, I can put more in this type of letter, so I'm continuing to send some of them this way. Besides it doesn't cost me anything.

Sunday I went on the tour to London and saw as much of the Tower of London as possible. There is so much history behind such a place it's hard to tell you all about it. It's a great old structure with 14 foot walls, moats, portcullis, outside walls, inside towers etc. Saw the Bloody Tower where poor Annie Boleyn was chopped and where a couple of Princes were murdered by Richard the III, where the Crown Jewels were kept at one time, the tower William the Conqueror constructed, where Sir Walter Raleigh lived and so on. You can see it was a very interesting outing and I enjoyed it very much. Dad'll have to come over here after the war with you, ma; he'd sure have a grand time looking over these places. There were only about 50 of us together, so our guide could give us lots of attention and answer all our questions. Gave me a little brushing up on my British history. I've certainly forgotten a lot, but it comes back fairly well.

Guess you'll be having good football weather now. Wouldn't mind seeing a game. I was lucky last year being at Long Branch and seeing all those good O.R.F.U. games. I love that game about as well as hockey.

Wednesday. *Lights went out before I was even nearly finished. To-day we're having a miserable rain but we actually had a few flakes of snow which was rather a nice change. Last night I had a pass so I went to Guilford to a show with my friend Bartholomew. It was an old show but the theatre was nice and warm so I enjoyed the film. My pal just got out of sick bay and has to get his tonsils out right away* [Ed Bartholomew was one of Bob's best friends and was with him in the fighting in Germany. He was killed on March 3rd in the battle for the Rhineland]. *We moved to another company to-day and he's left behind so I guess I'll have to find another pal to chum around. That leaves just one other former N.C.O. and I'm not particularly fond of him. However, we're all pretty well together here and we're getting to know each other better each day.*

Have read your last letter over many times. You do write the most interesting and nicest letters of any one, ma. I hope mine are half as good.

I have some Belgian money. I was going to send some to you for a souvenir but I haven't a small enough bill. Five francs is worth about one belga and a franc is worth about 2 1/2¢ in Canadian money. Am almost used to the English currency, but it's still very awkward.

This'll do for now. Expect to be elsewhere by the time you read this letter! Am feeling swell and thinking of you both very much.

Lots of love,

As Bob had hinted in the previous letter, he was on his way to the continent. His reserve unit was packed into a small ship with the men in hammocks, again in three tiers. Each man was given a paper bag in case of sea sickness since the Channel is notoriously rough. In their hammocks, the men were apprehensive and very quiet as the ship left harbour and soon began to be tossed about in the rough water. Bob heard the rustle of one paper bag, then another, as those around him succumbed to sea sickness (he had been wise enough to grab a top hammock). The punch line of the story was the exclamation of his next door neighbour (on the top tier) “Damn! My bag broke” and there was a general scramble as those beneath quickly vacated their hammocks!

The Essex Scottish Regiment and the Rhineland Campaign

On November 12, 1944, Bob saw the coast of Europe and began to experience the life for which he had been training for so many months, fighting the German Army and defeating Hitler. He also loved to travel, especially, as he often said, *"at the expense of the army"* and was eager for his first European adventure. He was to see action sooner than he expected, and was involved in the final Allied advance into Germany and the Rhineland. Bob was not able to say in his letters where his ship landed, but it was probably Ostend in Belgium, since Antwerp was not usable to the Allies until the end of November. He immediately wrote to his family and was able, at least, to say in which country he had arrived.

Somewhere in Belgium,
Nov. 13/44

Dear Mother and Dad,

I haven't heard from you for some time but I hope you are writing your usual letters and they'll catch up with me eventually. I hope you two are feeling as well as I do, because if that is so, you'll have no complaints. Can't say that the weather is what it could be though: still that misty rain. I don't seem to be able to avoid that kind of atmosphere no matter where I go—spring is coming, they say, so I shouldn't feel too badly there. Should be enjoying good wet Ontario spring by then, surely!

I sent my glasses home for the time being. I'm not doing much studying now and I'll manage without them and it wouldn't be long till they'd be broken. It seems like a waste of money, but they really helped me when my eyes were tired.

I wish I could tell you about some of the things I've seen and what I've done, but I know you understand. Later on I'll be able to tell you more. And with Jeff on my side, the Army will have no trouble holding its own against all comers when we have that great reunion at Inverhuron when this thing is over.

Belgium, where I am, is quite a bit like England's country-side except that here, it's very flat which I like, but also quite muddy and "lakey" which I don't like. The people are glad to see us, there's no doubt there, and it makes you feel good to see their faces and to feel so welcome.

I'm hoping to maybe see Jeff sometime while I'm in these parts, but haven't been that fortunate yet. What a meeting that'll be!

I'm afraid I must come to the conclusion that I'll miss Christmas with you this year. Oh well, I'll make up for it next year.

Love from your son -

On his arrival in Belgium, Bob was assigned to the Essex

Scottish Regiment, one of many replacements for the infantrymen killed, wounded or captured in the Normandy fighting. In the Essex Scottish, an infantry regiment, the authorized complement was 38 officers and 818 other ranks. However, as many historians have stated, the actual number of soldiers in a regiment in battle was often no more than half the total complement. There were four rifle companies (120 men each), the backbone of an infantry regiment, as well as anti-tank and other support companies. There were three regiments in a brigade and three brigades in a division. The Essex Scottish regiment was part of the 2nd Canadian Division.

In the War Diaries of the Essex Scottish in the National Archives in Ottawa there can be found a short history of the regiment (dated September 1944) which was given to new members. Bob would have received a copy of this document, reproduced below:

1st Bn., ESSEX SCOTTISH REGIMENT
Canadian Army (Overseas)

TO: THE NEW MEMBERS

You are now a member of the 1st Bn. Essex Scottish Regiment, and it is only proper that from the beginning you should know the history of your Regiment. This young but virile regiment has a fine record and one which every one of us has a right to be proud of.

From 1763 to the outbreak of the Great War, there

were strong militia units in Essex County and the neighbouring counties all of which in some measure are the ancestors of the present battalion. After the Great War, the 18th, 99th and 241st Infantry Battalions were joined together to form the Essex Fusiliers. This name was chosen as the unit was raised in the County of Essex, Ontario and in particular from the City of Windsor. The Essex Fusiliers under Lieutenant Colonel (Lt. Col.) Wigle remained an active militia unit until 1926. In this year it was decided to raise a highland unit. In 1927 the Essex Fusiliers became the Essex Scottish Regiment and the unit as we know it today was born. For the 13 years prior to the outbreak of the present World War, it was an efficient and strong unit in Canada's civilian army, the Non-Permanent Active Militia.

In September, 1938, the unit was mobilized for war under Lt. Col. A.S. Pearson. It remained in Windsor for eight months preparing for the battles to come. In April 1940, the unit moved to Camp Borden, as one of the units of two Canadian Infantry Divisions, to complete its training before going overseas. In July 1940 the unit sailed for England where it immediately moved to the South to take part in the defense of Britain against the threatened German invasion. Then commenced the hard period of waiting to come to grips with the enemy, carrying out its role summer and winter along the vulnerable coasts of Hampshire, Sussex and Kent but always training and preparing for the day when we would once again take the offensive.

In the early morning of the 19th of August, 1942, the chance came, for the battalion was part of the force which was to carry out the raid on Dieppe. The Unit under Lt. Col. P.K. Jasperson was one of the battalions which went in on the first wave assaulting the strong fortified defenses in front of the town. The story of the Dieppe raid is known to everyone. The courage and deeds of gallantry performed by the officers and men of the Battalion will never be fully known for many a brave man fell that day, his deeds of valour unwitnessed by the living. That the Unit acquitted itself with great distinction there is no doubt, for history has already recorded for posterity the glories of its deeds. Of 553 all ranks who embarked for this audacious stab at the enemy's heart, only 51 returned [the Essex suffered the most casualties of any unit at Dieppe]. Then began the task of building again this fine battalion to fight another day. This was accomplished and once again the Essex Scottish trained hard for another day and another chance [although the rebuilding of the unit took almost two years].

On July 4, 1944, the unit landed in France and immediately moved up to the front of the Caen sector where it engaged in the savage battles against the best the Nazis had to put against us, designed to draw all the enemy on to the British-Canadian front thus permitting the American Forces to take the Cherbourg and Brittany peninsulas. With this phase of the operation completed the battalion together with the rest of the Canadian Army turned to smashing the enemy on its front. Now, with the enemy reeling, the battalion strides forward, together with the allied armies, battling with all its strength and all its spirit to smash and utterly destroy the German Army.

The Regimental tartan is that of the McGregor Clan, chosen because its first Commanding Officer was a McGregor. The Regimental "March Past" is "Hielan Laddie". The Regimental motto is "Semper Paratus" or "Always Prepared". Here is a motto not one of us can ignore.

That then is the story up to date of one of Canada's finest regiments. You are now a member, and a very welcome one. Recall in the days ahead and in battles to come the record of your unit, fight with courage and with a stout heart, remembering always that you are the regiment and its continuing glory rests in your hand.

(P.W. BENNETT) Lt. Col.,
Commanding Officer,
ESSEX SCOTTISH REGIMENT.

The above "Welcome to New Members" certainly paints a glowing picture of the Regiment. What is not stated by Lt. Col. Bennett is the trial by fire that the Regiment underwent during that first month in Europe in the Caen area. According to the War Diaries, as written by Captain Fred Tilston on July 20, 1944, the Regiment had "suffered a disastrous defeat".

> *The enemy attacked the Essex position and three officers were killed, eight wounded and 140 other ranks wounded, and three officers and 130 other ranks were missing.*
>
> *It is not a pleasant picture to realize that so many of the battalion have been lost especially when the action was not successful and many of the casualties could have been avoided by better planning. All the rules of man management were either violated or ignored by the sudden move ordered after midnight, the loss of sleep by all ranks, a poor breakfast and little or no noon meal before battle and the general or detailed picture if known was not given to the junior officers or troops.*

The Essex was also engaged in the bloody battles of Falaise and Elbouef and, on September 3rd, reached Dieppe, the scene of the regiment's tragic 1942 losses, where flowers were placed upon the graves of the men who had died there. On September 9, the Regiment crossed into Belgium, and a letter written on September 13 by the commanding officer Lt. Col. Bennett to Colonel Prince in Windsor (Prince was honourary colonel of the Regiment) is reproduced below (from the War Diaries of the Essex Scottish Regiment: National Archives of Canada). It tells the story of the regiment's activities from Dieppe to Ostend in Belgium.

> *I was delighted to get your cable yesterday and realize from it the warmth of feeling and interest there is in Canada. As the weeks go by I realize more and more how fortunate I am in my command.*
>
> *My last letter to you was from DIEPPE and I now have the opportunity to tell you of our activities since then. From DIEPPE we moved in rapid stages into BELGIUM directed onto OSTEND. When we arrived there the Germans had fled after doing considerable damage. However we had another type of battle on our hands. The reception by the civil population was really beyond description. There is a large number of English speaking people there which assisted the fraternization no end. As we went up into the town the crowds surged onto the street waving flags, which they had made since the invasion started, cheering and shouting with the maidens taking every opportunity to express their joy by resounding kisses. I myself was not a recipient. Unfortunately in some ways we had to stop to deploy the battalion and they were immediately swamped. It was difficult to find*

any khaki at all amongst the seething civilians who by this time were running out with their long hidden bottles of wine and cigars of all things. It was a mad two hours before we got sorted out. Tailing the column were six prisoners who were the recipients of loud and long Bronx cheers all down the street. When we established battalion headquarters in a school we had to tape off the area and mount a guard to keep the crowds back. The battalion occupied the western outskirts to prevent any infiltration by the Germans trying to get out of the pockets further west. That evening the pipe band came and dressed in their kilts started down the main street of the town to play Retreat. They only got about six blocks when the surging crowd closed in and it was impossible to swing a drum stick or play the pipes. When I arrived the band was surrounded by 300 people who were dancing on the outside singing Belgian and English songs. Eventually the crowd started back towards the school with the pipe band lightly in their grasp. By encouraging the dancing and singing we were able to sneak the band out one by one, each member being clung to by three or four damsels who were deeply impressed by their physiques and kilts. I retired to bed early exhausted from the battle of OSTEND.

The next day, the 10 September, I moved out with the two coys (companys) and part of the sup-

porting arms to lay siege to a coastal gun posn, which was holding out just to the west in the sand dunes between WESTENDE-BAINS, WESTENDE AND LYMPARTZYDE. The civilians many of whom had worked on the posn (position) gave us detailed information as to the layout. Especially useful were two Belgian underground men who had everything in their heads in great detail. That day was spent finding the perimeter of the posn and pounding targets we could see. They had four old French naval guns as well as some arms. We exchanged fire all day with the Essex getting much the better of the duel.

The position itself was very strong. What had appeared to be sand dunes were concrete dugouts and emplacements covered with sand. The position commanded all the surrounding country. By the morning of the 11 September the whole battalion was on three sides of him with the sea on the fourth. We had some very good observation posts from where we fired our mortars, anti-tank guns and artillery. It was simply a question of picking out targets and then hitting them as hard as possible to knock them out as the place was a rabbit warren. Only occasionally could movement be observed and that when they came out of the ground to fire their guns or run from one position to another. The day was spent methodically knocking out what we could see and patrolling and sniping. They fired the big guns at point blank range without much success. That night we kept up the harassing fire, the 3" mortars particularly doing sterling work, and patrolling. We cut three gaps in the perimeter wire which was about thirty feet deep.

At first light we started shooting in earnest again and by this time we had some 17 pounders and some Bofors guns. By 11 o'clock in the morning he was really receiving quite a pasting from snipers, mortars, anti-tank guns which Jock MacLellan used with great skill, Bofors and artillery, all doing observed shooting. The 17 pounders and Bofors were getting shots right through the vision slits of the command post which dominated everything. We saw much more movement of personnel than on the previous day although little or no firing. I was around the companies all morning, teeing up patrols and generally making things as unpleasant as possible for him and returned to headquarters about 12:30 to fight the paper war and get a bite to eat. At 12:45 the phone rang from the OPs (Operational Position) to say white flags were appearing. This was a tremendous relief as an infantry attack against this position manned by a determined garrison would have been costly. I rushed up to the nearest OP to see twenty odd white sheets floating on the mounds and a German officer walking out with a white flag. From his French I gathered his commander wanted me to go in and see him. This I refused to do and Major Steele went back with him to bring out the commander, we meanwhile holding the officer as a hostage. Before the commander came out, the place began to swarm with Germans who flocked out of the main entrance. By now the local population was gathering in numbers. The commander came out and I accepted his unconditional surrender. While one company was dealing with the prisoners the others moved into the positions to search the area. Everything was of course underground and the battalion disappeared into the catacombs. The booty was absolutely terrific. From what I saw of the ammunition stock and food he could have held out for weeks. The quarters all underground were the most luxurious and filled with civilian furnishings of all kinds most of it taken from the villagers. As yet I have not a complete count of the weapons, but the prisoners totalled 316 including nine officers and 16 wounded. It was a wonderful sight to see them lined up. There was a good store of wine which Jim Watt and Al Gohen whisked out for the officers' mess and the M.O. (Medical Officer) got all sorts of medical supplies. Every man got a Luger or some souvenir and Doug McIntyre's company got the payroll of 107,000 francs. Very shortly we had the higher command down to see the place and everyone was very pleased with our efforts. I personally thanked God for this bloodless victory. Our total casualties for the whole show were two killed, three slightly wounded and Sergeant Dixon, who shot himself in the leg trying to find out how a Mauser revolver worked. His shame was unhidden for he has survived what no ordinary soldier could. He will never be allowed to forget it and I hope he will be back shortly. It is not a serious wound. I left one platoon from each company on the position to see no looting by civilians went on while the rest of the battalion withdrew outside the perimeter. The padre very early planted the Union Jack on the Command Post. That evening we buried Sergeant Riviat and Private Lyttle in the church yard at LYMPARTZYDE after the Pipe Band had played retreat. The whole village turned out for the funeral including the burgomaster and the priest. They have asked that the two men remain there in order that they may honour their graves and tend them in the years to come. We then repaired to our battalion headquarters with the burgomaster and the priest to drink and eat with the officers some of our loot of wines and food. The town clerk spoke English. Through him I told the mayor and the priest that we were most happy to have them with us to drink the wine of the Germans. The priest replied that he too was most happy as in all probability it originally came from his cellar. This rather shook me, but I decided I had not understood his reply and we all had a very good evening.

I arranged with the burgomaster to meet me at 9 the next morning at the enemy positions and I would hand over the food and clothes to him for distribution so all got a fair share. By the time I left there was a milling crowd at the entrance all hungry for loot. I do not know if his organizing ability will stand the test of this happy but hungry mob. Just before leaving I lowered the Union Jack and the Belgian flag was run up in its place. The burgomaster told me that they would rename the street running up from the position to the village "Essex Scottish Street". This I was happy to agree to.

The town clerk told me how impressed the villagers were with the relationship between our officers and men as opposed to the Germans. We are a very happy family, with what I am sure, has always been the same type of comradeship in the regiment. Amongst the loot is a large German flag which I am sending back to you as I feel it will make a suitable trophy for the mess in Windsor.

That is the end of my tale to date. Will you excuse the fact that the letter is mimeographed as I am putting copies in the War Diary? Time and the war goes on at such a pace it is difficult to find the hours in a day to do everything. I will in future send you two copies of my letter mailed on different dates in case one is lost in transit. The Pipe Band at this stage of the war is a tremendous asset to the unit and does much to maintain and encourage the unit spirit amongst changing personnel. In my next letter I hope to include a slate of officers with a brief history of each.

You are all very much in our thoughts. We had a wonderful shipment of cigarettes the other day, the first since landing in France, amounting to 100 cigarettes per man. These of course are like gold as soldiers are invariably short. The unit is in wonderful spirits and I feel we are not letting down the regiment in any way. Your kind and encouraging cable I am having put in orders for all ranks to see.

Yours very sincerely,

A second letter to Colonel Prince in Windsor dated September 20, 1944, is a very interesting account of the activities of the Regiment from Ostend to the area near Antwerp

Dear Col. Prince:

My last letter to you was written just as we were moving away from our highly successful action against the coastal battery near Ostend. First I

must thank once again, all our friends in Windsor for a further shipment of 75,000 cigarettes which have just arrived.

From Belgium, we moved back just over the border into France where we spent a peaceful two days in a reserve position. Battalion headquarters was in the ground of a lovely chateau surrounded by a moat. Here lived the Chocqueels, a fine old Royalist French family, who helped the B.E.F. (British Expeditionery Force) in 1940 and had their home shot up and looted by the Germans as a reward. The enthusiasm of the reception and their hospitality was incredible. "Mon Colonel" must have his "bureau" in the chateau. It was a lovely room. They were so kind and begged us to eat and drink what they had. For knives and forks they used British Army issue left by the B.E.F. as they had little else. They proudly produced a bottle of H.P. sauce which a Tommy had given them and which they had treasured. Our days were spent in catching up with the paper war — one can never claim a victory in this battle — and paddling the children around the moat. The night of the 15/16 September we left but before going we gave them a little party and presented them with an Essex Scottish patch and badge, backed by tartan. They were thrilled and could not bear to think of us leaving. They thought our soldiers were wonderful, so kind and so quiet. One German, they said, made more noise than fifty Canadians. Field Marshal Haig fought one of his battles from this house in the last war. We were sorry to leave, but too much inaction is not a good thing.

Our next move landed us on the northern outskirts of Antwerp. The trip up took us through Poperinghe, Ypres and Ghent. On the way, I went to Ypres where I saw the memorial gate and the damage done to it in 1940 as described by "bunbuster" in one of his books. The town is entirely new as is Poperinghe. On the way I broke away from the column and went to Passchendael. There were no signs of the terrific battles and on the ridge all we could see was cultivated fields and cattle.

Antwerp is a story of its own. We came in some days after it had been liberated by armor and the Belgian underground army who are a most efficient organization and really well organized. We drove through the town amid much enthusiasm. It has not been badly knocked about and to a soldier with a slit trench view of life, the place literally glittered. The cafes were doing a roaring business and the stores have plenty of luxuries and few necessities. However, it is like New York to a soldier from the wheat fields of Normandy. The enemy is not completely eliminated and it is possible to shoot at Germans on one street and move back a block and have an aperitif. It is all rather extraordinary. Antwerp celebrates its liberation while men are killed and wounded a mile away. But then it is a good thing. Who deserves more to express their joy than the suppressed peoples of Europe.

The battalion moved north through the docks to a position just south of Exeham, to protect the docks themselves. We are disposed in a series of military barracks houses and in large workers flats. The enemy opposition consists of shelling and mortaring and the occasional patrol. Since we got here 24 hours ago, and it is now the evening of the 17 September, we have had seven casualties including poor old Jock MacLellan, who was wounded again. This time I doubt if he will be back as he got it in the shoulder. We are hitting the German wherever we see him. Meanwhile we live in our solid apartments. Tonight we have heard that a large airborne force has dropped in Holland near the Rhine. What a well conducted campaign this is. I shall continue this letter at a later date. We have a Belgian with us of the underground army who tells a fascinating tale of his war during the past four years. No one can ever really know the true story of this wonderful spirit which has kept Europe alive. The sheer audacity is incredible. Tonight the pipe band played in Antwerp amidst a good crowd. They will play every night we are here. We can allow a small percentage into town each day which is a good thing.

The 18 September was an uninteresting day in the war. We have a no mans land of 2,000 yards which is flat open and waterlogged, and it is difficult to see enough enemy movement to warrant firing. There was intermittent shelling of our buildings all day but no casualties. The pipe band played retreat at 4:30 in the Cathedral Square in downtown Antwerp. The area was roped off with white tapes. There was a big crowd and all business stopped for half an hour. On conclusion, the tape was torn up by the spectators as souvenirs. "La Musique d'Ecosse" (bagpipe music) is a tremendous success. A form of ice cream soda and sundae can be bought which is quite an excitement amongst the troops.

The 19 September was dull and apart from exchanges of shells and mortars really little excitement on our front. However one can always find something of interest. I went down to see the pipe band play in one of the town parks. The crowds flocked to see and listen to the band. After each tune there was tremendous enthusiasm, clapping and cheering. There must have been 300 to 400 people there. The dividends were firstly a bouquet for the pipe major from a little girl, then an invitation to drink beer for the band and finally a free photograph in one of the studios for a piper Mackie and a drummer Moorhouse. I am sure the other units must be beginning to dislike us. It is a wonderful sight to see the band surrounded by people so joyful and full of enthusiasm. Young and old alike abandoning their cares and so ready to show their appreciation. I forgot to mention that yesterday I visited Jock MacLellan. He is having a pretty painful time with broken ribs and a bad shoulder as well as hits in his leg. He will be all right, but it is tough going for the present. Few of our wounded can bear the thought of leaving the battalion which is a gratifying thing...(The letter is continued by Major MacKenzie).

In the absence of Lt. Col. Bennett, who has become a wounded casualty, I shall continue and complete this letter. Just at dusk on the evening of the 20th, our relatively peaceful existence was disturbed by intense shelling on the part of the enemy. Very soon one company reported enemy on their front. From then on and for the next four hours, there was plenty of excitement. The company ably supported by artillery, succeeded in driving off this attack. Believe me, a shell exploding against a building is ten times as noisy as one which lands on the ground while one is comfortably squatting in a slit trench. And at night the darkness likewise seems to expand the noise of battle to an extraordi-

nary extent. The particular night in question was a very dark night. It was during the early part of the fracas that Col. Bennett received a nasty leg wound. After having the wound dressed, he refused to be evacuated and stayed at the command post until the enemy attack faded out some four hours later.

In the absence of Col. Bennett, and so long as I am permitted to remain with the regiment, I shall continue his practice of keeping you informed of our activities. With kindest regards to all our Windsor friends, I remain—

Yours very sincerely

(D. MACKENZIE) Major
A/Officer Commanding,
1st Battalion, ESSEX SCOTTISH REGIMENT.

Although Major MacKenzie promised to write further to Windsor about the activities of the Regiment, no more letters were found in the War Diaries. Perhaps the new C. O. Lt. Col. Pangman felt he had little time for letter writing. By November 8th the Regiment had reached Groesbeek in Holland, 8 km south east of Nijmegen (see Map 2) and only 3 km from the German border. There was scarcely a house intact in this town, and only a few goats and sheep wandered around the ruins.

Among the Essex Scottish men, there was a very strong feeling of attachment to the Regiment. There is no doubt that the Essex, along with the Royal Highland Light Infantry, had more

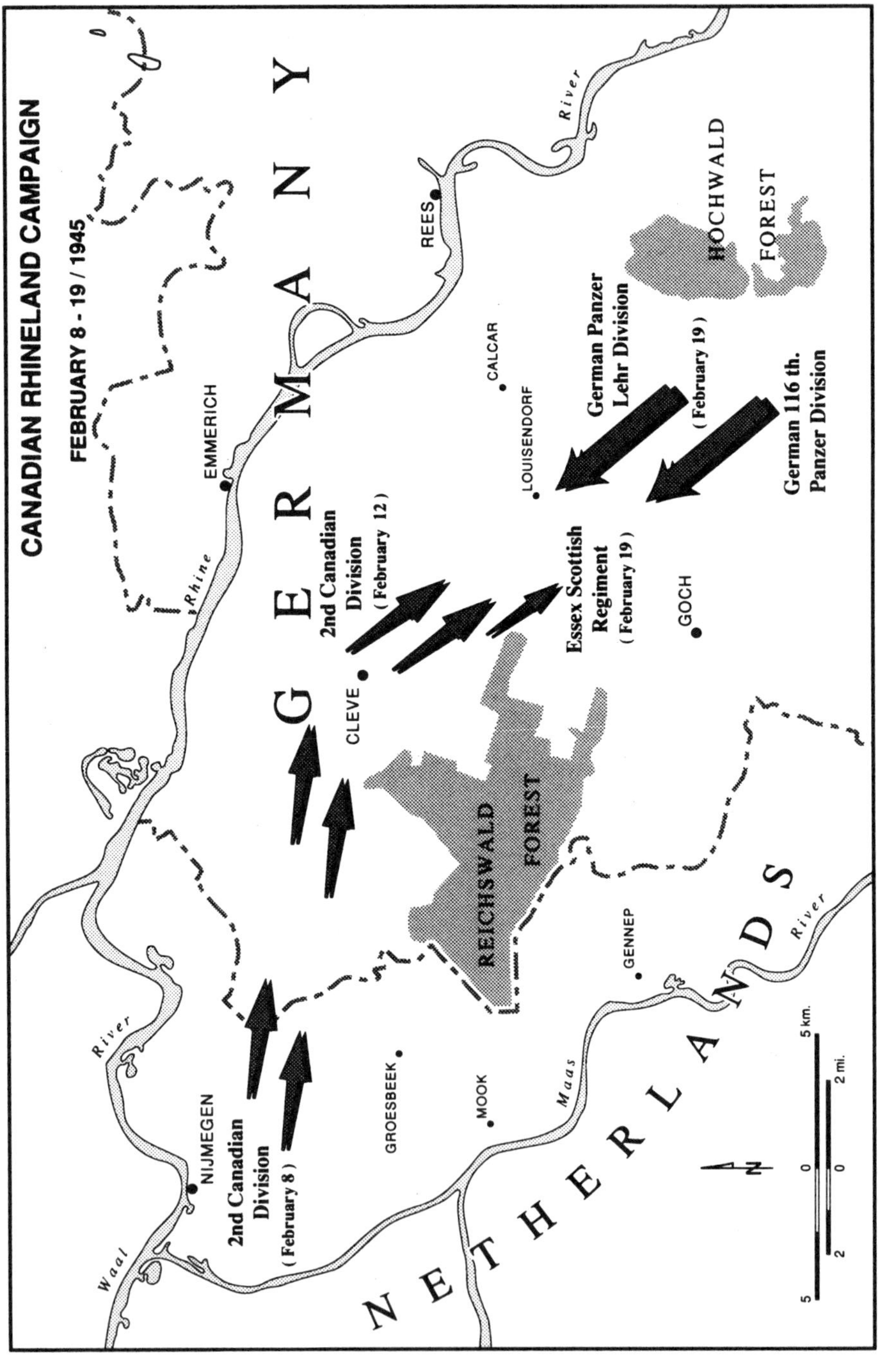
CANADIAN RHINELAND CAMPAIGN
FEBRUARY 8 - 19 / 1945
GERMANY
NETHERLANDS
Rhine
River
Waal
River
Maas
River
NIJMEGEN
GROESBEEK
MOOK
GENNEP
CLEVE
EMMERICH
REES
CALCAR
LOUISENDORF
GOCH
REICHSWALD
FOREST
HOCHWALD
FOREST
2nd Canadian
Division
(February 8)
2nd Canadian
Division
(February 12)
Essex Scottish
Regiment
(February 19)
German Panzer
Lehr Division
(February 19)
German 116 th.
Panzer Division
5 km.
2 mi.
5
0
2
0
N

Map 2

than their share of the work and the tragedies of the Rhineland battles. Bob's next letter is the first bearing the name of the Essex Scottish.

Fri. Nov. 17/44
Essex Scottish Regiment

Dear Mother and Dad,

Well, it's somewhere in Holland now and all is well on the Western Front! Am writing this by candle light, so I must hurry before it goes out.

Hope you two are looking after yourselves. I'm glad to be in this Essex Scottish regiment. I hoped it would be this one and was lucky there. I'm in the 2nd Division.

Slept in a barn last night in a pile of straw with two other boys. Had blankets and was very comfortable in my boudoir. Had a grand sleep. Very glad to have had my summers up in Northern Ontario. Comes in handy to know what to do these days. [This was a reference to his camping experience and his ability in "roughing it"]

Hope some mail comes in soon. The people here are very good to us and treat us wonderfully at least as well as their means provide. Very quaint with their wooden shoes and plus fours. (some of them). Their houses are all good buildings (usually brick) and really nice inside—not like England in that respect.—much like home.

Was all through a windmill where they ground grain and was very interested. Building was 100 years old and still going strong. Rainy and cold weather is still the vogue here too! —but that doesn't surprise me.

Am thinking of you two and home often and am very lucky to have such a swell place and swell parents to think about. Please don't worry about me.

Lots of love -

Bob joined the regiment on November 15 in Groesbeek in the Nijmegen area in Holland (see Map 2) where the chief job given to the Essex Scottish was the holding of the vital Nijmegen bridge, the only bridge over the Rhine still intact. The regiment had spent the night of November 8th in convoy. The men had moved on foot to the village of Groesbeek where they were billetted in cellars, and Bob joined "B" Company in its quarters in a coal cellar. Here he met many of the soldiers who were to remain his friends—among them Walter (Pete) Heaton, from Harrow, near Windsor.

Pete had enlisted in the Essex Scottish in Canada in 1943, when he was only 18 years old, because his older brother while with the Essex had been captured at Dieppe. Pete joined the Regiment in July 1944 near Caen and was immediately involved in battle. He was wounded with shrapnel in his back and sent to England to recuperate, but he was back with the Regiment in October. Bob's other friends in his platoon were Bill Wilson from Toronto and Al Goggins from Windsor who was always called "Pop" (since he looked older than the others although only 22) and Bob Sallows who looked about 14 years old, but was actually 18.

Private Pete Heaton, Essex Scottish

Pete recalls that his first impression of Bob was his arrival—all "spit and polish" and clean shaven and with a clean uniform—to the coal cellar during shelling from enemy mortars. One of the recollections Bob had of that day was of the mortars (called Moaning Minnies by the men) which the Germans were sending into the area. The sound of the bomb (the moaning) gave the soldiers a few seconds to find shelter and Bob found it most amusing that, when they heard the moaning, some of the men ran outside, while those outside ran inside, usually colliding in the doorways!

Tues. Nov. 21/44

Dear Mother and Dad,

Someday I'm going to get on the mail list and get all your news. It shouldn't be long, now that I'm in a regiment. When you are in a reserve unit, and moving, it's hardly possible for any letters to reach you.

It's good to be in a regiment as I said before. I've followed this one in its travels and escapades more than the others since I knew some of the men before and also because it is a Windsor outfit. I haven't met up with many of the boys yet but I know that there are a few men from around home. There's a Van Slyke from Hanover and Gobert from home. Was talking to a chap by the name of MacLean who went to school in Chesley and Dad taught him. Guess they're all over the world, eh Dad?

(It is now Wednesday). Army duties come before writing,

of course, so I had to set this aside for awhile. It's too bad you can't see me these days. I've a bit of a beard, including my ragged moustache, which still gives that slightly Chinese appearance, and am a wee bit on the dirty side. The bristles are just a bit too long and my face is beginning to itch so I'm hoping to get cleaned up soon. I can easily imagine how Jeff felt when he said it was wonderful when he got that first bath after so long. Jeff is not so very far from here but haven't had any chance at all to get near him or his unit.

Bob didn't have much time to become acquainted with the Regiment, but almost immediately was living in trenches in the front lines. The "duties" he mentioned were the reconnaissance patrols into enemy territory that the Essex were engaged in. The purpose was to find the location of the enemy troops and to take prisoners, if possible. He and Pete Heaton often went together on the patrols. These were usually at night and it was dark, and usually raining, and they often were lost. In addition, the rain on their rain capes made so much noise that they couldn't hear anything at all. Once a cow came up from behind and touched him on the shoulder. It could have been a German soldier! Bob quickly realized that it was a matter of life or death to remember the password. Each day the password was changed and the soldiers on patrol would keep repeating "juice" (if the challenge were "apple" for example). It was difficult to know who was friend or foe in the darkness.

As for me, I have no needs to suggest for you for

Christmas. Meals are not bad but, of course, a box wouldn't ruin my appetite. Send some batteries for my little pen light. A few cigarettes would come in handy too. Guess that's about all I can think of at present.

The progress of the war seems to be very favourable so we are all hoping it'll continue so we can get the job over with and get back where we belong doing what we like. One of the first things I'm going to do when I get near a restaurant is order a nice cold glass (a big one) of good cow's milk and a toasted bacon and tomato sandwich. Oh, man, what a snack! It'll be a great day. Catsup would of course be within reach.

Will write again as soon as I find that necessary time. Everything is under control and I even think I've gained a little weight.

All my love,

On November 23rd, the Regiment de Maisonneuve took over the Essex Scottish position in the front lines and the regiment withdrew to a reserve location in the village of Mook on the River Maas. The town was badly destroyed also, but at least the regiment was not in cellars, as in Groesbeek. Passes were issued to Nijmegen— a prosperous and attractive city although quite damaged and crowded with refugees. Here some recreation, as well as training and reorganization was possible. The daily routine was reveille 0630, roll call 0800, training parade 0815-1200, dinner 1200, training parade 1315-1615, supper 1630 and tattoo (with pipe band) 2300.

B. Company, Essex Scottish Regiment
Thurs. Nov. 30/44

Dear Mother and Dad,

Haven't much to say, but have a few extra minutes and can drop you a few lines. Had a nice shower and a good shave to-day so I feel quite "tiddly" right now. Also put on a full quota of clean clothes that I had packed away so I am very comfortable.

This morning I attended a communion service which the padre of our regiment arranged for us. It was a very nice service very much like the ceremony used in the Anglican churches back home and I was very glad to go. Our padre is a Capt. Joe Cardy and is very well liked, being quite young looking and just like one of us. [Captain Cardy was later awarded the Military Cross for his work with the Essex Scottish]. *Last Sunday morning we had our church service in a renovated Dutch pub, I believe it was. But the place doesn't matter and the message the padre gave was a very good one and I enjoyed it very much.*

Am becoming more acquainted with the members of my regiment and platoon and am liking it fine. The R.C. padre was just in this writing room of ours and gave out some tasty food. It sure was good. When you send a parcel be sure you have some cheese and some sardines in it somewhere. Fruit cake is always good—and chocolate bars are a great delicacy and a luxury.

One thing about the front's rations is that the stew has little or no onions so I'm managing very well at meal times—but no cat-

sup. Start salting those bottles away. Often think of those Sunday feasts we had back home. We boys were spoilt I think. You looked after us too well but we loved it.

Am managing to have plenty of cigarettes. The City of Windsor sends the regiment some from time to time and the supply is coming in very well at present. The other day we were all given our rations and I benefitted by two large packages of Sweet Caporals (that's a cigarette brand, pop) on a trade so I'm doing ok. By the way, I prefer Buckinghams if anyone is wondering, but I'm not too fussy.

My mail has not yet come through, so enough said there! Hope I get some before this war is over. "Jerry" is beaten but I guess it's his hope to prolong the war so he can get out of unconditional surrender—but that's not our idea of a settlement.

Am thinking of you both very much and miss you but it shouldn't be too long till we'll be having that roast beef dinner with all those trimmings and your sons will be trying to convince you what branch of the services really won the war.

Goodnight,
Look after yourselves,
Love from your Army son

By December 1st, the regiment moved again to a forward position and the men lived in dugouts—muddy and cold. There was real danger of "trench foot" caused by prolonged standing in cold water, or the continued wearing of wet socks and boots. Pain was the first symptom, and then the foot became cold, numb, swollen and red. The best prevention was to change socks often and the men were each issued four pair.

On December 2nd, the Germans cut the dikes on the south side of the river at Arnhem and there was extreme flooding. There were extensive German fortifications in this Rhineland area—the area between the Rhine and Maas Rivers in Map 2. The German defences were arranged in three lines, the first east of Groesbeek, a second inside the German border west of Cleve, known as the West Wall or Siegfried line, and the third east of Cleve, and south-west to the Hochwald Forest. These lines of defense were well fortified with mines, trenches, barbed wire and anti-tank ditches.

Bob often mentioned that, after his weapon, the soldier valued most his spade. As soon as their position was obtained, the soldiers lost no time in digging a "slit trench" which might be 5 ft long, 4 ft deep and 2 ft wide. Here they would "live" until relieved. If they were lucky, the company cooks would bring hot food to the trenches at night. Often this wasn't possible and the infantrymen subsisted on their canned rations. These slit trenches were often located among the gliders still in the area from the September operation Market Garden. The gliders offered protection for the Germans who often threw grenades over the gliders into the slit trenches.

The weather was cold and wet, and life in the trenches was certainly not comfortable. The soldiers lived for their time out of the lines and the hope of mail from home. The next letter (Dec 4) indicates that it had been six weeks since Bob had left Canada and his first letters caught up with him only on December 3rd.

B. Company Essex Scottish Regiment
Somewhere in Holland!
Mon. Dec. 4/44

Dear Mother and Dad,

Just a short note to let you know I got a letter from you yesterday. It was forwarded from Debert and you wrote it Nov. 6 so my mail has found me and things should be better from now on.

Since I was only in England for three weeks, it was impossible for me to get any pictures taken. I have a fair moustache now and wouldn't mind having a picture taken of it (and me all around it) but can't very well have it done here.

I'm sure the parcels will reach me eventually with the address you gave. The boys here are getting quite a few parcels and I'm being very well looked after by them. Good bunch!

It's getting dark now, so I must close for now. Will write again soon. When you wrote that letter I was already in England since I landed in my camp there on Oct. 21st.

Love from your youngest son

B. Coy. Essex Scottish Regt.
Tuesday, Dec. 12/44

Dear Mother and Dad,

Well, since it is getting near the 25th I am wishing you a very Merry Christmas and the best for the coming year. I hope this letter reaches you at the right time. My thoughts will be with you particularly on that day and by the time the next one rolls around surely we will have it all together with Dad supervising the Christmas tree proceedings. I don't think any family had a happier Christmas day than ours. I hope that if your sons were unable to get home for the day that you went to Stratford. They will find their Christmas different this year too, and I'm sure you would enjoy it at Prestons.

Last Wednesday I had a surprise visit from Jeff [cousin Jeff Preston]. *He came over to see me in his jeep and we had a grand chat for awhile. He is certainly looking well, I believe handsomer than ever, and seems to be looking after himself very well.*

My watch has arrived and I am very pleased with it—my Christmas present, I call it. It's just what I want, and I've been lost without one since I sent my other one home.

I got two boxes of chocolates the other day so I've received my first parcels—one from the Ladies Association of your church, and other from Women's Institute. I've written them already to thank them for their gifts. (Was going to say, send bigger box! but didn't, rest easy, ma).

Had our first snow Saturday, so we'll undoubtedly be having a white Christmas. Our dugouts leaked so we had a time when the snow melted, however, everything is very snug now. Monday we all got high rubber boots and I was very glad to get mine as were the others. When your feet are dry and warm, comfort is usually yours. Right now I've no complaints and all is fine with me.

Love to you both -

Major Jeff Preston, Cameron Highlanders

The problem of keeping their feet warm in the slit trenches was one the soldiers had to contend with during those cold winter days. One method was to remove the Army boots and socks, and, seated opposite a friend, massage each others feet until the circulation was restored. The cold was so severe, often -20°C, that many soldiers suffered frost–bitten feet. It was wonderful to get out of the slit trenches and be warm for at least a while. On December 15th, the Essex regiment was again relieved by the Regiment de Maisonneuve and returned to Mook where they remained until the end of the month; part of the time in buildings and partly in trenches. A regimental dance with 300 men was held at the Wintergarden in nearby Nijmegen on Dec 18th, as Bob describes in the following letter.

Sun. Dec. 17/44
B. Coy, E.S. Regt.,

Dear Mother and Dad,

Just got off a special guard duty at 4 to-night and Jeff drove up in his jeep so we've had another little visit. Sure is great to see him now and then. He's having a few days so-called rest too so was able to get over to see me. We are only a few miles apart—(kilometers, we have here, but I'm not used to figuring distance with them yet). Jeff casually told me he had a promotion—a major now, in charge of one of the companies in his regiment. Congratulated him. Am sure he deserved it—they don't come any better and he has what it takes for a company commander.

Before he left we made each other feel good! I hit him a good one—I've always wanted to let a major have it! Course you know Jeff, he pasted me one and said "I've always wanted to hit a private!" I held myself back though, and didn't hurt him too badly, so we still parted as happy cousins.

Think about the best feeling I've had over here yet was when I saw two Jerry planes knocked out of the sky. Sure was a great sight and I loved to see those Nazis go down in flames. Sounds a bit gruesome—but as long as they're Nazis—the more the better.

Am enjoying the comradeship in the platoon more as each day goes by and we have a swell bunch here. You were wondering if I'd found a chum. We're all chums over here—no particular one. Living together as we do, we all became very close and are all "pals". I'm with the best bunch of boys that I've met up with in the army, so you see, I'm quite happy and very lucky! [Bill Wilson of Toronto was one of his special buddies, and he survived the war. Al Goggins also survived. Bob Sallows was killed on March 8th in the battle for Xanten, the last phase of Operation Veritable].

My parcels haven't come through as yet, but the others in my section are getting them regularly and we're always having something extra to satisfy our palates. They look after me in cigarettes too. I'll have a lot to pay back, but, of course, they don't think of it that way.

<u>*Continued on Tuesday. Dec. 19*</u>. *I still have this letter so I'm adding a few more lines.*

Was at a regimental dance last night [This was in

Nijmegen, although he couldn't say so in his letter]—*First dance since I was at Debert—except one dance I had in London. It was a nice change but I can't help but say that I was a wee bit disappointed in the Dutch girls present; I think they were attracted to another dance nearby and it made the girl situation a little grim, however, I had a couple of dances and some fun anyway. Have been in Nijmegen a few times for relaxation and have had a little look around and saw a few shows put on by the army services.*

I can tell you now that I landed at Liverpool when I came overseas. I was not sick on either of my boat rides although one day I was a bit light in the head. It was really rough that day and many boys were not so lucky! I have not yet been in France in my travels, but one never knows.

Can't help but think of your being alone for Christmas. I do hope you were able to go to Stratford. It would be so much nicer for you both. We're having our Christmas party to-morrow night—which naturally consists of extra rations of special food.

Love again -

On December 16th, General Rundstedt who was again commanding the German troops on the Western front, had launched an offensive in the Ardennes against the American sector and British troops were rushed south to assist. Just before Christmas there was widespread concern over a possible German attack and indications of a build-up of German troops on the Nijmegen front. From documents obtained after the war, it is known that three German infantry divisions had been assembled with the objective of capturing Nijmegen. However, the attack never materialized.

On December 23 after three weeks in reserve, the Essex Scottish, expecting the attack, were moved into a front line position relieving the Queen's Own Cameron Highlanders and its tasks were to provide standing and, on occasion, reconnaissance patrols. The forward companies were in close contact with the enemy, the area being only about 2 km west of the Reichwald forest. Bob was in the front lines on Christmas Eve which was a clear moonlight night and it was a strange feeling to hear the German soldiers singing Christmas carols, the sound carrying clearly over no-man's land. It certainly made the Canadians homesick. On December 25th the Essex moved again, this time to Nijmegen and on the 29th to Boxtel, south of 's Hertogenbosch where they were billetted in an agricultural school.

During the final months of 1944, three Army groups of two million men were massed near the German border along a 600 mile front. In the north, in Holland, General Montgomery was in command of the British and Canadian troops that faced the Ruhr area. Montgomery suggested two simultaneous assaults on Germany. "Operation Veritable", a thrust from Nijmegen by the British and Canadians under General Crerar, was planned to take place between the Maas and the Rhine, south-eastward toward the Reichswald Forest. In the south "Operation Grenade" under American General Simpson was to thrust north-eastward to link up with the Canadians and British troops. This was to be the beginning of the great "Rhineland" offensive that would, finally, take the Allies into Germany, but it did not take place exactly as planned.

B. Company, Essex Scottish Regiment
Sat. Dec. 30/44

Dear Mother and Dad,

Have been rather unsettled lately so haven't written for awhile but now I'm quite comfortably writing to you on my stomach (no desk around) and even have electricity to light my way.

Thought of you on Christmas and hoped you had a happy day even though the war has kept us away this year. This year I had to more or less satisfy myself with those happy memories of our other Christmases together and I really had a good time whispering to my chum about it. Guess your other sons were doing much the same thing but we'll make up for it next year.

To-morrow night is New Years Eve. Sure has been a busy year for me—with all my travelling. Guess it hasn't been my happiest, but no one's been happier in the army than myself and that's what counts, eh what? Had too many good years before this army life that can't be beaten by this job. Guess it is the same with everyone over here.

Your parcels haven't come through yet but should be along soon. When you send another could you include a couple of face cloths and a bottle of shaving lotion, my face gets rather irritated when I take off my beard and I think the lotion will soothe it a bit. Have lots of blades.

Weather here isn't too bad and at least there is no mud at present and the ground is hard with no snow in most places, but it's cold enough, particularly at night.

Haven't had much chance to look over the civilians here, but I do see a few around at times. We have very little to do with them. Some parts of Holland are rather close to Germany, you know, and pretty close neighbours. You mentioned something about these people possibly being able to do some of my washing. Not much of that done for us, but others in different circumstances are well looked after in that respect—such as the artillery men and armoured corps and R.C.A.F. [Royal Canadian Air Force]. *I won't tell you how long I've had this underwear on or when I had a bath, so I do sort of need one. There are showers in some vicinities, but we haven't been able to lease them lately.*

My watch is still working perfectly and I've had several offers to buy it. One was for 100 guilders (about $42) but what would I do with all that money—and no watch? Money doesn't mean much to me. I may get a leave in February sometime or March and it may come in handy for that 48 hour holiday, but that's a long way off. I have about $50 in my pay book which has accumulated from month to month, so if I do get a leave, I won't be without funds.

Lots of love -

On New Year's Eve, the Germans launched an attack on the southern (American) flank of the Allied lines, while the Canadian segment was comparatively quiet. New Year's Eve was one of little hilarity in the Regiment although Fred Tilston in the War Diaries tells of:

> *"a lad in a tank corps hat—shoulder flashes of another unit who peppered the streets with a Sten gun. When apprehended he gave as his excuse that no one had told him not to do it—which somehow reflected the sense of responsibility abroad in the world as the year ended".*

And on New Year's Day the Pipe Band played in the streets of Boxtel, greatly to the joy of innumerable children.

A-106266 Sanderson R.M.
B. Coy, E.S. Regt.
Wed., Jan 3/45

Dear Mom and Dad,

Just got your letter written Dec. 24 so thought I'd drop you a short line or so.

You were wondering if I needed gloves, a sweater or such. I'm pretty well looked after there at present. I was without gloves (lost, strayed or stolen, of course) for a long time after leaving the boat in Belgium but managed until Marie sent me a swell pair— with leather palms and on insides of fingers. I was very glad to get them and they're so much warmer than the others. I have that nice knitted sweater the Institute gave me, yet, so I'm well provided for there, too. You could send me a pair of socks, now and then but I'm ok. there also at present. There's not much point in having excess or too much extra for it will only be lost or mislaid— and the biggest point (lazy me) it means more to carry. The more mobile you are, the better, and we can only carry so much.

There's no snow here where I am and the ground is frozen, so no mud—which, as I said in my last letter, I think, is quite to my liking. The weather is quite cool but we only wear our greatcoats when out at night so you see it isn't the same winter here as you are having at home—so far. The longer it holds off the better we all like it.

Did I tell you I bought this snazzy writing paper from a Dutchman a couple of days ago? He owns a paper factory and has some surplus he could sell to us. It's pre-war paper, he said. It cost 2 1/2 guilders (about $1.00) so it should be good stuff. It isn't bad anyhow and I needed it for my writing booklet.

Remember that woolen skull cap given to me by the Ladies Institute to wear under my helmet? Well, it's just like my "shootin' iron"—always with me and my best pal. It sure is a handy thing and I wear it all the time, day in and night out. It makes the helmet fit on the head more comfortably and is certainly just the thing for me.

My New Year's day was much pleasanter than Christmas. Nothing special, but the atmosphere (you know) made the big difference and that means more than anything else over here. [He meant that New Year's day was not spent in slit trenches]

Well, folks, all for now: everything fine here and no big complaints to make so all's well.

Love from son -

On January 5 the Battalion moved north to the town of Vught where a monastery and other buildings in the town were taken over, but the stay was a short one, and on January 7th the Essex again returned to the Nijmegen area. "B" Company (Bob's company) occupied a position on the right flank of the Canadian position, "D" company in the centre and "A" company on the left, with "C" company in reserve. Left of the Essex were the RHLI (Royal Hamilton Light Infantry called Rileys) and the Royal Regiment of Canada (Royals). Patrols were sent forward to determine the location of the German troops. The weather was bitterly cold with temperatures again in the -20°C range and a cold wind out of the north-east.

B. Coy. Essex Scott. Regt.,
Tuesday, Jan 9/45

Dear Mother and Dad,

It's been a few days since I last scrawled a few lines to you so to-night the lights are working well, we have a nice fire going and everything is very satisfactory for fixing up my correspondence situation—which by the way, is very bad. I'm very much behind in my letters. Although I have very little that I can tell you, I try to write you just about as often as I can.

This week end we had quite a snow fall and with the weather as cold as it is, it has stayed with us. I know you'll be wondering how we're managing in this type of weather. The big problem is how to keep your feet warm on certain nights, but we manage.

Good news! I received your first parcel last week. It was

Box #2. Your first hasn't found me yet. It was swell box, ma, and thanks a lot. I sure enjoyed it and my pals did too. The honey was a grand treat and please thank Mrs. McC. in case I don't write her for awhile—also the delightful chocolates. It was very good of them and I shall remember them for thinking about me. Everything arrived in fine shape. The chocolate drink is a treat with everything prepared in it. If I can't get any water, I just take a spoonful and it tastes good, even that way.

I'm back around Jeff's way again, so I may be seeing him sometime soon when he finds out where I am.

Well good night -

Love

The Germans had achieved such important gains in December that the British War Cabinet, in its meeting on January 12th, suggested that the war might not end until December 1945. Meanwhile, however, the Russians had launched a massive attack in the east, advancing to within 60 miles of Berlin. On January 12th, the Essex was back in the front lines, with "B" company on high ground overlooking saucer-like country which rose in the east to the Reichswald. As before, the chief task of the Essex was reconnaissance patrols to try to find the location of enemy troops. Usually at night, these involved four or five people and the purpose was to keep the enemy conscious of the Allied presence, and to take prisoners if possible.

On one of these night patrols, Bob and Pete were requested to report to Captain Fred Tilston, who was later to become the most famous of all the Essex Scottish officers and receive the Victoria Cross. The two became lost in no-man's land, Bob suggesting one route and Pete one in the opposite direction. Luckily they decided on Bob's direction since Pete's suggestion would have taken them directly into the German front lines. They were an hour late reporting to Headquarters and to Captain Tilston, who said *"Why are you late?"* and Bob answered *"We were lost"*. Tilston showed his sense of humour when he replied *"Well, boys, the next time start out an hour earlier, so you will arrive on time"!*

There were also five "standing" patrols of Essex Scottish men during this period of cold weather in January. The men occupied these positions at night and it was difficult to keep warm as Bob mentioned in his letter of January 9th. Most of the action occurred at night, when there was a good deal of enemy movement.

Jan. 17/45
B. Coy, Essex Scott. Regt.

Dear Mom and Dad,

Am afraid I'm a bit late in writing but I think you'll understand my circumstances and believe my good intentions.

A few days ago I had supper with Jeff. We had another get together at his headquarters. As you can imagine there was a great meeting—almost as momentous as the ones Roosevelt, Winston, and Joe have. We had a swell meal together and got caught up on each other's news. We were very fortunate. He's sure a grand cousin. That crown on his shoulders doesn't make him any different. I saw his girl's picture and I think he's doing o'kay. Congratulated him and he agreed that it was about time. [Jeff was engaged to be married]

I got a parcel from Aunt Flo and managed to get a short thank you letter to her. Was a lovely box as usual and we enjoyed it very much. That's two boxes I've received, so they are finding me ok now. I sent you a pair of clompers as a bit of a souvenir of Holland. Not much, but I don't get much chance to do any "shopping".

Things are the same here. Weather is fair with the usual cool evenings. Lately it has been milder than usual and that suits us as you can imagine. We have white snow suits which we wear on certain jobs and they're really wonderfully warm and quite ritzy.

Hope you are both well and happy and enjoying the Chesley life. Take it easy and lie in bed in the mornings and read a good book. Boy,—that'd be the life—for awhile anyway! Right now, I don't think I could get enough of that sort of life,—only I don't think I'd bother reading—if you get what I mean.

Much love to you both

The night of January 21st saw a reconnaissance party shot up by an enemy patrol— one killed and three wounded. The next night a whole section (eight men) which had occupied an outpost position, was captured and a relief party found no trace of the men.

The final days of January were crisp and cold with sunny skies, and the patrols were provided with the white camouflage

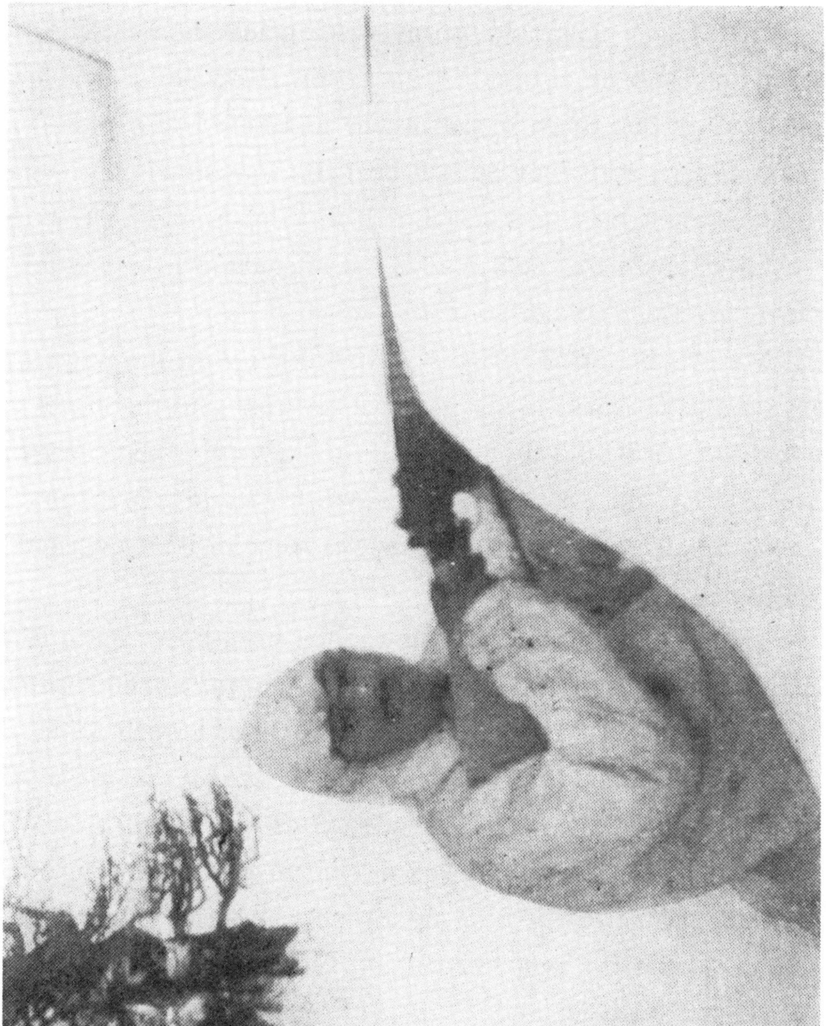

Essex Scottish soldier in the front lines, Jan/45.

suits (which made a man almost invisible against the white background) that Bob mentioned in his letter. Bob never told his parents that on one of these patrols, he and Pete had captured a German soldier, and after he had been interrogated, they were ordered by their officer to shoot him. It was impossible for Bob or Pete to shoot anyone in cold blood, and after the officer had left, they let the German soldier go free.

Morale among the men was improved with the news of successes by the Russians on the Eastern front and there was a hope that the war would soon be over. In full view of the German lines, the Essex men erected signs saying "Russians Welcome" and the Germans retaliated by firing over some of their own propaganda.

The rest of January was spent in the front lines, and a full moon made patrolling at night difficult. There was an increase in enemy movement, and the soldiers could see the German soldiers *"wandering around with full equipment on as if a change-over had taken place"*. On the Allied side, the front seemed to be on the verge of boiling over, and it was evident that something big was brewing. There was little opportunity to write letters until February 2 when B Company was moved back to C Company dugouts for rest and clean up.

Sunday, Feb. 4/45

Dear Mom and Dad,

It isn't that I haven't been thinking of you lately, that I haven't written, but one must have reasonable conditions and time for writing, as you know, and I just haven't been able to get around to it.

I got a letter from you to-day as well as one from Fred and so I'm squeezing a quick letter in now. I hope I have time to finish it to-night. I was amazed and delighted to get the letter from you two with Dad's characteristic handwriting addressing it as well as his note inside. Good going pop: It's one letter I'm going to try and keep somehow!

Since last writing to you I've received your boxes up to #5 so I'm beginning to be spoilt in that regard—also two from your wonderful little sister. All were very much enjoyed and they couldn't have come at a better time. We've been on Compo rations [These were tinned rations which the infantry was given when it was impossible for them to leave the slit trenches to return to the area where hot meals were served] *for some time now and the extra delicacies certainly hit the spot. Also received a pair of glasses which I wear over my other ones and they're just the thing for my job.*

The Enterprise is coming in quite regularly now and I digest its contents with a careful eye. It's a great paper for a Chesley boy to get and I'm one who appreciates it very much.

It didn't take me long to decide that I'll continue my Canadian way of living and they can continue and keep their European ways. It would be different if conditions were slightly revised, but even so—there's no place like Ontario, believe me.

Still no 48 hour leave for me yet but should have one very soon. Am looking forward to it very much and will probably go to Brussels—not likely lucky enough to go to Paris.

Weather is mild (moderately) and the snow has disappeared in a recent thaw so our dug-out homes and slit trenches are a "wee" bit on the wet side. Have it fixed up pretty well now and if it leaks it can darn well leak!!

Well folks! Gotta do a spot of work for awhile and I've just time to address this—Thanks for those boxes ma. The cheese spread was grand, also the socks, which I'm wearing now.

Much love from your youngest

The preparations for operation "Veritable" were going on at this time, but no direct confrontation with the enemy had yet occurred. The Canadian and British build-up for Veritable was enormous—1,000 guns, seven divisional artilleries, two anti-aircraft brigades and massive air support. One thousand heavy bombers were to completely destroy the German towns of Cleve, Goch and Emmerich before the land battle began. Of course, the infantry privates never heard the plans for "Veritable" or any other operation. They were told each day what the objectives were for that day, and tried to do their best to attain them.

The German general, von Rundstedt later admitted that he had not anticipated such a large scale attack in the Reichwald area, but felt that the main offensive would be in the south in the American zone (Operation "Grenade"). This "Grenade" offensive which had been planned since November was to be delayed by General Simpson, since the River Ruer which they must cross, was in flood. This resulted in dire consequences for the Canadian attack in the north.

Feb. 6/45

Dear Aunt Florence and Uncle Jim,

Your letters have been coming in fine and it's good to hear from you. Your last took only eight days so I'm really quite up to date on the news. I've found it rather difficult to write letters lately but I managed a letter home to mother yesterday and when I finish this one to you I'll have the most important letters looked after.

I received a lovely parcel from you last week and it sure hit the spot. Thanks for everything including the swell socks. My supply of them is fairly good but I can always use them. I can only carry a couple pair with me and they really just came at the right time to replenish my supply. I hope I thanked you for the Christmas parcel you sent me. It arrived only a couple of days before the other one so I guess I didn't. Everything arrived in good shape and at just the right time to be appreciated the best—both of them.

Sometimes our appetites fail us when it comes to the same "compo" rations every day and the extra delicacies were just the thing for us. In fact mother's parcels have been catching up to me of late and I've really been spoilt with parcels and my diet has been rather wonderful.

Things here are under control and our dugouts are quite comfortable. A recent thaw has taken all the snow away and there is a "slight" dampness about but not too bad really. Have been hoping to have a 48 leave sometime soon, but they're very slow in finding my name, unfortunately. Am looking forward to it very much. Have been in action three months now so leaves as you notice aren't quite the same as back at Ipperwash.

Often think of you two and hope all is well with you. I can't even catch a cold to get a day off, so you see how well I am.

Much love -

February 7th was spent in an increasing state of alert on the part of the Essex outposts and there was heavy traffic on the supply roads. The details of Operation Veritable were announced. The War Diaries for February 7th stated:

> *"The strength of the forces and equipment massed for the attack seemed staggering and our ring-side seats for the big show seemed to make up for the long period of inactivity on our own front. We were not included in the initial phase of the operation. Personal messages were received from Montgomery and General Crerar and read to all in the battalion.*

February 8th was D day for operation "Veritable". The task of the Essex Scottish was to draw the enemy into the artillery fire line. The night of the 7th, 700 bombers of the Royal Air Force destroyed the towns of Cleve and Goch, not far away inside the German border, presenting an awesome spectacle for the front line troops. At 5 a.m. the next morning a thousand guns hammered at the German defences. "Veritable" was designed to overcome the Germans' three defensive lines between the Maas and the Rhine rivers which were described earlier (see Map 2). Beyond the third lay the Rhine itself.

The weather did not co-operate. During January, with the cold weather, the ground was frozen and made vehicular movement easy. However, in early February there was a sudden thaw and the roads became so muddy that many of the vehicles became bogged down. It must be remembered that in those days, most of the roads were not paved. In addition, because of the opening of the dikes in Holland, the main road from Nijmegen to Cleve was flooded, just where the main thrust of the attack was to take place.

The purpose of "Veritable" was to destroy the three lines of German defences west of the Rhine and advance into Germany. The second and third Canadian divisions were involved. Air support was massive and the amount of equipment brought to the area was phenomenal (eg. 35,000 vehicles and more than one million gallons of gasoline). General Montgomery called "Veritable" a memorable battle which in intensity and fierceness equalled any which the Allied troops experienced.

The enemy's resistance at first was disorganized and confused, and the first day of battle carried the Canadians into Germany, where they captured 1,300 prisoners. In the next few days, however, the battle grew in violence as the Germans brought in reinforcements. In the south the U.S. Operation "Grenade" did not begin as scheduled and was delayed two weeks, permitting the Germans to rush their troops northward. This meant that "Veritable" continued alone for two weeks and the enemy could concentrate his reserves against it.

On February 12th, the regiment was moved again to

Nijmegen where they were dry and fairly comfortable in a block of Dutch barracks. On February 14th, Valentine's Day, a dance was held for the troops. On the enemy front, on February 10th, the Germans had brought in the 6th Parachute, 15th Panzer Grenadiers, the 116th Panzer and the fresh Panzer Lehr divisions. The Panzer Lehr alone had 22 tanks, 3 battalions of infantry, a reconnaissance battalion, an engineer company and an artillery battalion. These seasoned German units, now fighting on German soil for the fatherland, displayed the courage of despair and fought with ferocity and determination. The battle for the Reichswald area, in which the Essex Scottish was involved, was considered by army historians to be the fiercest fighting of the war.

Feb. 14/45

Dear Mother and Dad,

I think to-day is Valentine's Day or thereabouts to my way of figuring and I didn't send any valentines to my best gal, ma. Hope you'll forgive me this time; I'll try to do better next year. I didn't send any valentines, so you can't be a bit jealous now.

There isn't much that I can write about as usual—security you know, but things are rolling very well on our side now and everything is under control. Jeff will be back with his regiment by now and his bunch are doing very well too. Those Russians are really giving Jerry the works, and they're just the ones who know how to do it the right way. Have seen quite a few of these "super-duper" men and when they haven't weapons in their hands they're a pretty decrepit and beaten bunch. Have seen plenty of prisoners so it is quite evident they don't all listen to the paper-hanger and Göring!

We've been very busy now for quite a while and get pretty tired sometimes which is quite natural. Letter writing does relieve one's mind, but sometimes a few winks of sleep is more enticing when we have some time off.

Got a new battle-dress to-day; my other one was in pretty bad shape so I feel very dressed up. Also got a hair cut. Was quite a shaggy looking individual with six or seven weeks growth.

I was next to go on my 48 hour leave but I'll have to wait awhile till the leaves start again. Am I disgusted!!

(Am finishing this on the 15th.) Your parcel arrived ok to-day with bulb and batteries for flash. Sent Dec. 29—but I've lost my flash. Can you get another of some kind. More trouble, eh? Thanks for the swell scarf sent in a former parcel. It's really nice and soft and I wear it all the time—even at night. Pretty nifty for my job here.

Much love to you both -

The city of Cleve had been taken by the Allies on February 12th and on February 16th the Essex was moved in tanks into the town, their first venture into Germany. Here they were installed in the basements of buildings still undamaged, but the general impression was one of utter destruction. At 6.30 on February 17th, final timings for the offensive "Veritable" were issued and the unit moved to an assembly area between Cleve and Calcar. The objective for the Essex Scottish, and the Royal Highland

Light Infantry on their left, was to capture and hold the Goch-Calcar road. Each regiment was to be supported by 16 tanks of the Fort Garry Horse. The area was an open area dotted here and there with farmhouses and sheds.

Bob knew, of course, that the fighting would be fierce and he knew, also, that he might not survive this next battle. He had been in the front lines since mid–November and had not been wounded. But he did have a close call, which he hadn't told his parents. After one night patrol, he discovered that his first field dressing, which is attached to the outside of the helmet that every soldier wore in battle, had been pierced by a bullet. Since the Essex Scottish had lost quite a number of men, Bob was again given the rank of Lance Corporal whether he wanted it or not, as he stated in his next letter.

H–hour for "Veritable" was set for 1500 hours on February 17th, but at 1350 word was received that the attack was to be delayed. The next day was foggy and miserable in the slit trenches as the regiment waited for the word to attack. This gave Bob a little additional time before the offensive, and he wrote letters to not only his parents—but to cousins Jack and Marion Preston and an uncle and aunt (his mother's brother and sister-in-law).

Feb. 17/45

Dear Mother and Dad,

Just a short note to let you know all's well and going fine. To-night I'm sleeping in an air-raid shelter in Germany [Cleve].

We're really quite comfortable. The shelters are about the only things left that are usable.

About my work—I'm a section commander now and am liking it not too badly. Wasn't going to take any stripes or be an N.C.O. again but I've changed my mind, I guess.

Germany looks the same as any other place, but pretty badly damaged where we are anyway. Just had a feed of German canned cherries and fruit of all sorts and they were really good—so they aren't a starving nation by any means. Am using a German envelope—pretty snazzy—eh?

All for now—much love
Army son

Feb. 18/45

Dear Jack and Marion,

I must tell you that I'm writing this manuscript in Germany. We've been living rather well as far as grub is concerned as we move along, having the odd(?) chicken, and porky that we manage to catch. Stray ones, of course, and we're only borrowing like they did in Russia, Holland, Belgium, etc.

All's going very well anyway and we're hoping that Jerry will see the lights of democracy very soon.

Haven't seen Jeff since he got married. There are a few from his regiment nearby but they're from a different company.

Have had only one 36 hour leave since I left Ontario and that one in London so you see I haven't had much opportunity for fraternization with foreign girls till now. However, I was in Ghent for a few days quite awhile ago and at least saw a few anyhow. That city is a wee bit on the wild side—too wild for me—you know me.

Well must close for now. To-morrow being rather a busy day, so I must get as much "schlopen" (sleep) as I can. Being a section commander I don't have to do any regular guard duty at present so I'm lucky there.

-Bob

Sunday, Feb. 18/45

Dear Uncle Art and Aunt Dot,

It has been some time since I've written you now and my location is a bit different from back in Canada. I've been intending to write you two particularly since seeing your son with Jeff some time ago. A couple of days ago a grand parcel arrived from you and I may be a little busy sometimes but I must let you know it arrived in good shape. It has been looked after already in that typical Sanderson manner and my pals join in with me when I thank you for it. My mail and parcels have been finding me in quite good time lately and they are appreciated more than usual these days.

I'm in Germany as I write this and I get a great kick out of writing letters in Hitler's home of super-duper men. Things are going along very well and it seems just a matter of time till Jerry sees the light!

Things aren't too bad these days as far as weather is concerned—at least, the rain has let up a bit, but the mud is still rather bad—and German mud is pretty bad.

This'll have to do for now. Thanks again.

I'm a mighty Lance Corporal now, by the way! I hope you and Aunt Dot are well. I haven't even a cold!

"Luff and kisses" -

The next day, February 19th, was to be a crucial one in Bob's life and the day that the war ended for him. There were three infantry platoons in Bob's company (B Company) which was commanded by Major Frank Chauvin. B Company's objective lay in the little town of Louisendorf (Map 2) where they were to place a platoon across the highway south of the town. In the War Diaries the "Essex Order of Battle" was the following:

Infantry in Kangaroos [Kangaroo Tanks]	—	left A Company
		right B Company
On foot	—	left C Company
		right D Company
Rate of Advance	—	100 yards—1½ minutes

Armed wave to go straight to objective, shooting up as they advance.
Infantry wave - by pass opposition to reach objective.
Mop-up by Royals [Royal Regiment].

Part of the official report of the engagement described in the history of "The Essex Scottish Regiment" as written by Captain Rob Meanwell is given below.

> *"The morning of February 19 dawned cloudy and mild. At 10:30 the Battalion moved off to cut the Goch-Calcar road near Louisendorf with the A and B Companies moving into position on Kangaroo tanks.* [The Kangaroo was a tank with the gun removed to transport troops into battle. It usually carried about 12 men]. *Infantry men hated to be transported in tanks thinking that at any moment they would be hit by enemy shells and incarcerated in the tank. C and D Companies were on foot to clear the ground once the armour had passed. The Essex was supported that day by those squadrons of the Fort Garry Horse tank unit.*
>
> *H-hour was noon and the momentum of the attack carried the lead companies to their objective in good time. A and B Companies dismounted from the tanks and fought on foot under a hail of small arms fire and grenades. Major Chauvin was wounded early in the battle and taken prisoner. Casualties were heavy. About 1500 hours the enemy counter-attacked."*

Louisendorf, Germany—where the author was taken prisoner, Feb. 19, 1945.

It was not known, of course, to the Canadian Army in the Cleve area that opposing them were the men of the crack 116th Panzer division and the Panzer Lehr Division. The 116th were called the "Windhund" or Greyhound division and it was one of the most famous of all German divisions. It was named the "greyhound" because one of its generals had taken a greyhound dog into battle in the 1942-43 campaign. Success after success was gained by the division. They had blocked "Market Garden" at Arnhem and stalled the Americans in the South. In January they fought in the Ardennes. Now they were brought in as the key defence against "Veritable". They were elite troops. The Chief of Staff of the 116th Panzers was Heinz-Guenther Guderian, the son of the famous Heinz Guderian, Chief of the German General Staff in 1945. He said later of his troops and their ferocious fighting *"They were not fighting for the Nazis, but for the Fatherland"*. The Panzer Lehr Division was another of the elite German tank units. It had just arrived in the area from the American sector to the south when it became obvious that there would be no major offensive by the Americans.

Captain Meanwell in his official report of the Essex Scottish continued:

> *"The might of tanks and infantry launched repeatedly against the Battalion made it difficult to maintain the position. The right flank bore the brunt of these attacks, and the failure of a British division to secure ground to the Regiment's right earlier in the day because of a cancellation of their*

> *plan, threw a great burden on the Battalion which was not originally intended for it."*

In the Essex War Diaries, there is a hand drawn map of the company positions. It can be clearly seen that Bob's company (B Company) was completely exposed on the right and first to be overrun by the enemy. Many years later in the Whitakers' book ***"Rhineland"***, Major Charles Barrett was quoted as saying that *"the Essex were being overrun because their right flank was exposed . . . On February 19th, we had a liason officer from the British at the 4th Brigade HQ and we asked him for the position of his troops. They were supposed to be coordinating their attack with us.*

After we'd launched the attack, word came back that the British hadn't moved, they hadn't gone into the attack at all. I remember, at the time, I was really shocked to hear this. We asked them why they hadn't moved, and their general or brigadier, or whoever it was that was in charge of that unit, said that he felt we could handle the situation on our own. But he never told us that he wasn't going to move. To my naive mind, I thought that was a terrible breach of conduct and discipline."

To continue with the Essex Scottish history:

> *"Communications were poor or failed altogether. Vehicles became bogged in the soft mud. Casualties were difficult to evacuate. Tanks and anti-tank weapons did not reach company localities*

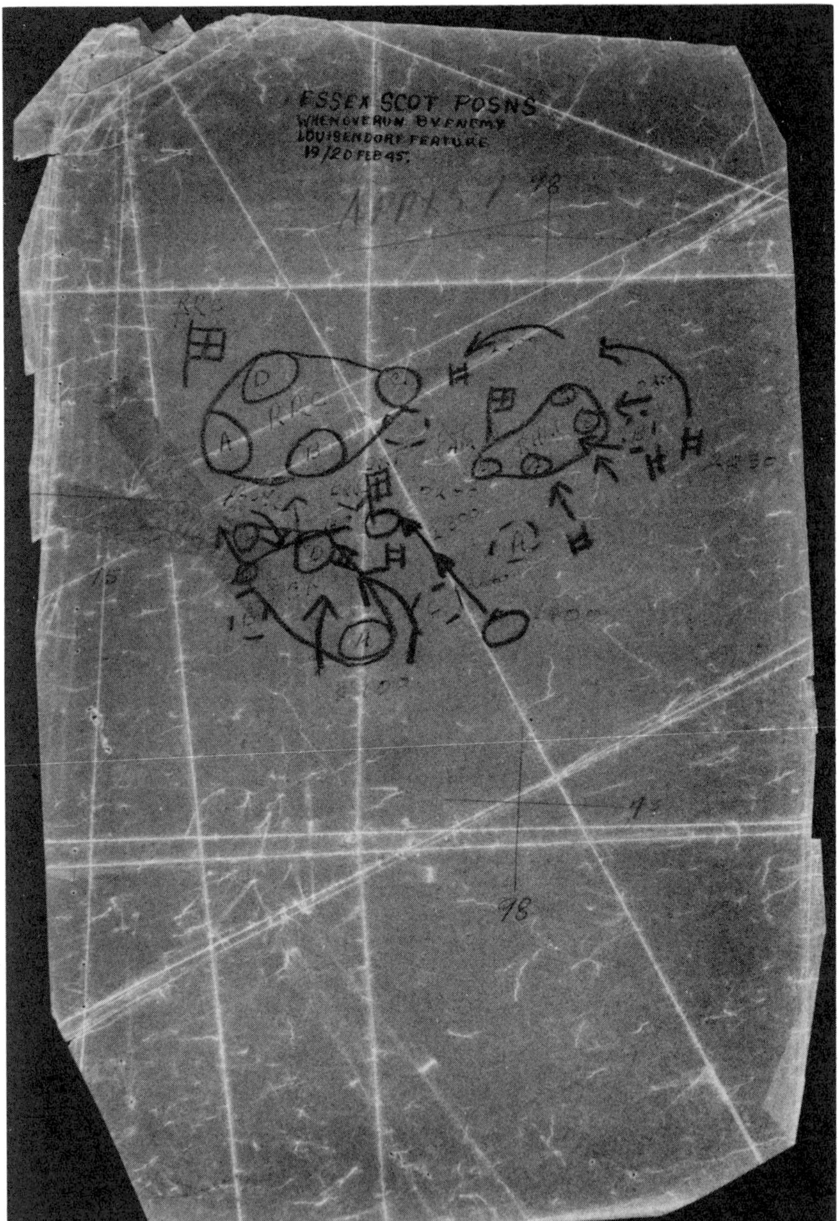

Field map of Essex Scottish positions 19/20 Feb. '45.
(Courtesy National Archives of Canada)

and ammunition could not be brought up when required. Darkness fell and the efforts of the enemy continued. After midnight, communication between tactical headquarters and the rear link wireless set stopped, and for hours nothing was known of the fate of the command group, and much was feared for its safety."

The War Diaries of the Essex Scottish noted:

"The early hours of the morning were grim. Isolated company groups fought on, short of ammunition, burdened with casualties which could not be evacuated . Back in the assembly area, the reports from the Battalion were extreme difficulties, intense enemy counter attacks and severe casualties on both sides.

As day dawned, the Regiment withdrew from the battle-scarred ground to shake itself and lick its wounds. To hold off the enemy and to present a breakthrough had taken more from us than we wished to remember. As the remnants of the companies returned to the assembly area, steps were taken under Captain Tilston to reorganize and re-equip.

The battle, which was later to be called the battle of the Goch-Calcar highway continued until February 23rd when an attack on the RHLI and

RRC (Royal Regiment of Canada) was repulsed and some prisoners taken".

Final casualty figures for the regiment for this battle showed 13 officers and 235 other ranks. Fifty men were taken prisoner and the final accounting showed 46 killed in action.

Back in Canada, the Sandersons had no letter from their son since the one dated February 17th. Then came the telegram that every parent dreaded from the Department of National Defence, stating that Bob was missing in action. This prompted the newspaper article that is reproduced facing page 1.

Waiting for news of a son must be one of the worst war experiences. Bob's mother wrote to everyone she thought might have some news of that fateful February day—or have some connection with the Essex Scottish.

At the end of March they received a letter from Europe from nephew Jeff, who with the Cameron Highlanders, was engaged in the Canadian Army's push into Germany.

Major W.J. Preston
14 March 45

Dear Aunt Nellie and Uncle Stanley:

I just received mother's letter written from Chesley. I am terribly sorry to hear about Bob and know how you feel about him being missing from operations.

Well, we were right near Bob on February 19th but I never

got the chance to see him. I saw their attack go in and everything went fine. They did come under some very heavy fire. At night Jerry counter attacked and their position was over run. Bob was with his section and they were the forward ones and "caught the packet". They did a marvellous job and it certainly has been the toughest fighting since the early days in the beach head.

When I heard of the counter attack, I immediately contacted the regiment and they only knew he was missing. We had to wait a few days until we moved into that section and I could look around. I contacted their regiment again and they still had nothing further to report. We eventually relieved them and another unit in that area so I personally searched the battle field but could not find any trace of him. However, I will try to get in touch with his unit again and see if they have anything more. It is impossible to say what has happened but I sincerely hope that he is a prisoner-of-war and in good health.

The Canadians have been doing a wonderful job and, as I said before it is the toughest fighting since the early days over here. It is the tough, stubborn fighting that got us to the Rhine.

Well, I am sorry I could not write sooner but had to wait until you got official word from the Government records. I will keep in close touch with his unit and let you know.

All my love
Jeff

Meanwhile, Bob's Uncle Hardie in Windsor inquired of his friends in the Essex Scottish, and received the following in April from Major Ken MacIntyre of the Essex Scottish. [Major MacIntyre was later awarded the Distinguished Service Order for the part he played in the Goch-Calcar battle].

1 B in The Essex Scottish Regt.,
Canadian Army Overseas
5 April 45

Dear Hardie,

I was very pleased to hear from you, but naturally regret that it had to be in connection with the report of your nephew, Bob Sanderson being missing. On our attack 19 Feb., I was commanding A Company and naturally can give you no first-hand information regarding Bob, but the information I have is from the clerk of B Coy and is authentic in as far as it goes.

The attack on 19 Feb. was an armoured drive and the fighting was bitter and confused. Bob was seen by the members of B Company debussing from an armoured vehicle near the company objective about 1230 hours on the 19th. No other details are known about his activities from then on. He was in #11 platoon which was split into two attacking groups, one commanded by an officer who was killed; the other by a sergeant who was surrounded and evacuated.

The particular battleground was regained about 48 hours later and when searched failed to reveal any trace of your nephew.

Consequently, he is assumed to be missing and is likely a prisoner of war. We can only hope that he was not wounded and is safe in an enemy prison camp somewhere. From all reports the Germans are treating prisoners well. Let's hope that he will soon be reported as an official prisoner of war.

If there is anything else I can do for you Hardie, please let me know.

We have crossed the Rhine and are now fighting and chasing Jerry around in Holland. My batman, who had been with me for over a year, was wounded in the foot yesterday morning. I'll keep my head down, as you suggest! I'm now second in command of the regiment.

Sincerely,
Ken

Finally, Bob's mother received a letter from the Department of National Defence dated April 9/45, but it didn't give the reassurance his parents hoped for—that their son was indeed alive, and a prisoner of war.

Ottawa, Canada

Mrs. Nellie P. Sanderson,
Chesley, Ontario

Dear Mrs. Sanderson:

Further to our telegram March 2nd, 1945, and letter March 5th, 1945, in which your son A.106266, Lance-

Corporal Robert Miles Sanderson was reported and confirmed missing in action, I am to advise that the following information has been received from your son's Unit in the Field.

"A.106266 Lance Corporal Robert Miles Sanderson was last seen by his Platoon Commander then engaged with the platoon in clearing buildings of the enemy. Lance Corporal Sanderson was last seen advancing with his section at about 1230 hours February 19th, 1945. The Platoon split into two groups to attack the enemy position. The group with which Lance Corporal Sanderson was advancing came under enemy small arms fire and when the objective was finally taken Lance Corporal Sanderson was missing. He was in danger of being taken prisoner as at that time he was within enemy territory."

It is regretted that further information is not available at the present time regarding the fate of your son but as no trace was found of him it appears quite possible that he may have been taken prisoner; however this cannot be regarded as official.

You may rest assured that when further definite information is received, you will be notified without delay.

Yours truly,
W.H. Armstrong, Capt
for (C.L. Laurin) Colonel,
Director of Records,
for Adjutant-General.

The waiting continued. Because of the rapid advances of the Canadian Army and poor communications in Europe, the Sandersons did not receive further information about their son from the Army. Finally a letter arrived from an unlikely source, from Canadian nursing sister Mary McCulloch sent on May 6th from a hospital in England.

Dear Mrs. Sanderson,

I received your letter of April 30th yesterday and am so glad you wrote me. I will do my best to get what information I can regarding what Major Chauvin has to say about Bob [Frank Chauvin was the Major of B Company in the Essex Scottish and was wounded and taken prisoner on February 19th, then repatriated to England and was a patient in her hospital]. *I was past his room last night but the door was closed and so I didn't like to barge in. However, I'll see him when I make my morning rounds. I have been talking to George Hepburn from Chesley. He came in as a patient two days ago. I mentioned Bob to him. George is with the Royal Reg't of Canada and apparently they were working in coordination with the Essex Scottish at the time of this particular attack. He was talking to Bob the night before he was reported missing but, of course, that was the last he saw of him. According to George, Bob had been at the time of attack with A company although you say he had been in B company which is Major Chauvin's company. However, I may be mixed up regarding that but that is comparatively unimportant anyway. Major Chauvin remarked on the outstanding courage Bob had displayed and cool headedness. He said that he was an exceptional soldier and had he not been taken prisoner definitely would have received credit probably with a promotion* [This was the first real news that Bob's parents had that he was a prisoner of war]. *George Hepburn said Bob had refused it several times when offered it and during their chin wag on their last visit together joked about them wanting to make him a corporal and he wouldn't accept. Guess I had better leave a little room for what remaining information I can collect.*

(Sunday 8 a.m.) Just came back from seeing Major Chauvin and I'll corroborate whatever I have told you before. Bob was in B coy. The reason you heard from the officer in A coy. was because the officer in B coy. was taken prisoner or killed. Major Chauvin was himself a prisoner. Hence the only one left to report to the boys' families was A coy officer Ken McIntyre and he therefore signed the report that was sent to you. Walter Heaton was one of the five remaining alive. Apparently Walter received some sort of facial injuries from a bomb blast and will probably lose his left eye as a result. This Walter Heaton is released now and should be on 14 days leave. Major Chauvin had been talking to another one of the company that seemed to know. He suggested that unless Bob had been wounded he should also be on leave so perhaps by now you may have heard. I think that is all the news I have to report. Will let you know if any further details are forth-coming.

I can quite appreciate how anxious you will be. Wishing you all the best.

Sincerely,
Mary

Although Bob's parents were pleased to receive this letter, they still had no official word that their son was alive. They wrote to Pete Heaton's and to Frank Chauvin's parents for any possible information.

Pete Heaton has told me what a good officer Major Chauvin was. He led B Company into battle that February 19th, and was wounded in one leg. He was captured and treated in a German hospital where his leg was amputated, and because of this, he had been repatriated by the Germans to a hospital in England. This was why he was able to pass the information about Bob through Mary McCulloch. Major Chauvin was later awarded the Silver Star (USA). He subsequently returned to Windsor after the war and became a successful and well–liked lawyer. But his post–war years were few. He died when only in his forties.

Bob's account of the events of that February 19th was not received by his parents until May when he finally wrote from England.

On February 19th the Essex went in on regimental attack at 11.30 a.m. "B" Company, my company, went to its position in Kangaroo tanks. We immediately dug our slit trenches near the village of Louisendorf. We came under heavy fire and by mid-afternoon I was the only N.C.O. of our platoon left and all our officers in our company were either killed or wounded, except my own officer who had to take over the company. He told me to take charge of what was left of our platoon and prepare for Jerry's counter attack. He counter attacked (and how!) but we held them off till late in the afternoon. By then we were cut off from what little there was left of our regiment and out of ammunition. We were pinned down by Jerry's fire all around us but we hoped to hold out till night time and make a run for it. However, we learned later that we had ridden (on the tanks) about two miles into the middle of a German Panzer division which was just ready for an attack only we had attacked first [the crack 116th Panzer and Panzer Lehr divisions]. *When he brought up his tanks we had nothing to fight them with, except our small arms weapons—and a few grenades. Well, Jerry used a ridge to creep up on us and managed to throw a shower of grenades and bazooka bombs at us. Quite a few of the boys had "had it" by then and this was the finishing touch. There were four of us still ok. but then Pete received a grenade which blew him out of the slit trench and he started wandering around in no-man's land.*

Pete Heaton has told me that their situation that day quickly became impossible. There were farm buildings in the area and some of the Panzer troops were on the roof of one building. From there they could shoot directly at the men in the slit trenches, as well as throw grenades at them. The soldiers called these grenades "potato mashers" since they resembled an old fashioned potato masher—with a long wooden handle. Bob was at the time using his Sten gun and managed to kill quite a few of the enemy before his ammunition gave out. [Bob was always very reluctant to tell this part]. Pete himself was busy looking after a signals officer, who had been hit with a grenade and fallen on top of Pete in the slit trench. Pete gave him a shot of morphine when a grenade exploded on the officer, killing him instantly. A second grenade landed in the slit trench and Pete threw it out, but a third exploded in his hands. It blew him out of the slit trench into no-man's land as Bob stated in his letter.

I remember saying "My God, they got Pete". I got out of the slit trench and ran to him and tried to patch him up. [Knowing Bob's background, there was no other action for him to take—to try to save his friend's life at any cost]. *That moment I consider my second birthday since I was looking right into the muzzle of a German Schmeisser held by a German soldier on a Tiger tank, but the Jerry didn't shoot. Why I will never know. I told the rest of the platoon to follow me and Jerry was in a capturing mood as you've found out and there's the story why your son became a prisoner. I sometimes wonder just what would have happened if Pete hadn't been hit! It seems like a bad dream now—but parents, I wasn't a bit afraid. I don't want that to sound boastful, but it's a fact.*

Maybe I shouldn't be writing all this stuff, but that's what happened and how I felt. I learned later that our regiment had suffered rather high casualties and had been pretty badly broken up but were re-organized and went in on the attack again a week later.

During that terrible afternoon, the enemy mounted seven counter attacks against the Essex Scottish and at about 6:30 in the evening, B Company's entire position was overrun. The files of the German Army reported that the Panzer Lehr had been ordered to counter attack at 1416 hours, and the attacks continued through the night of February 19th, the Germans infiltrating as far as the battalion headquarters of the Essex Scottish and the Royal Highland Light Infantry. Meanwhile A Company, under the command of Major Ken McIntyre held out in a farmhouse until February 21st, when the order was given to withdraw. Fierce fighting continued for the next ten days, but by the evening of the 21st the Essex had recaptured the Goch-Calcar road. The Panzer Lehr division was sent south in anticipation of an American attack, and by February 26th Operation Veritable could be said to have ended. In the ten weeks of fighting, there had been horrendous casualties, the Canadians suffering almost 1,800 while the German forces had 12,000 killed and 11,778 captured.

March 1 saw the Regiment reorganized and in the front lines once more in the Hochwald forest area. That day's engagement became famous in the history of the Canadian Army and the Essex Scottish because of the personal bravery of Major Fred Tilston for which he was awarded the Empire's highest award, the Victoria Cross. He was wounded in the head and in the hip during the battle but carried on until a third wound in the leg forced him to accept medical attention. He subsequently lost both legs. His Victoria Cross citation read "By his calm courage, gallant conduct and total disregard for his own safety, he fired his men with grim determination and their firm stand enabled the Regiment to accomplish its object". Canada lost one of its heroes when Fred Tilston died in September 1992.

The regiment continued the attack into Germany and captured the ancient Roman town of Xanten on March 8, after fierce fighting. By March 24 the Allied Armies crossed the Rhine and on May 8 the message was received to cease all offensive operations. For the Essex Scottish and all Canadian troops, the war was over. Late in September, the Essex moved to England for final leaves before embarcation for Canada. It returned to Canada one of the most decorated units in the Canadian army. The final tally of the Essex Scottish showed 552 fatalities (37 officers and 515 other ranks). Of this number, 5 officers and 46 other ranks had been killed on the single day of February 19th near Louisendorf.

The following paragraphs were taken from a diary in which Bob wrote in the prison camp after liberation.

I was captured on February 19th, at 5 p.m., along with Heaton (wounded), Jensen, Bonham (wounded), Dent (wounded), Wilson, Moose MacDonald (Fort Garry Horse Major, who had taken cover in our slit trench when his tank was blown up), leaving a signal officer in the slit trench dead of wounds from grenades. There was no one else alive from B Company. The men who were not wounded carried the wounded, since the alternative, to leave them, would have meant almost certain death. (We also heard stories that the Germans were shooting all prisoners but the Jerries in the Tiger tank didn't shoot us).

We were then taken to a barn after being searched at a farm house where we tried to patch up Heaton and Dent. That night, Moose MacDonald said he would try to escape, which he managed to do, and made his way back to the Allied lines.

Pete has told me that he remembers parts of these happenings, although he was often unconscious. He remembers that Bob and Bill Wilson carried him into the farmhouse where a German first-aid person bound up the worst wounds. Here Bob and Bill Wilson put Pete on a door to carry him, since they were told they would have to walk to a barn where they would spend the night, but finding this too awkward and heavy, carried him between the two of them. Pete recalls saying *"Put me down and let me die"*. This of course they refused to do. They spent that night in a sheep barn and each Canadian was interrogated individually. One of the questions was *"How did you get into this area so quickly"?* [They didn't know about the kangaroo tanks]. The Germans were planning the counter attacks and needed information on the Allied units opposing them. Of course the prisoners, according to the Geneva Convention, were required to state only their name, rank and serial numbers. This they did.

Finally Bob and the others were taken away and a German ambulance took Pete to a hospital. Pete doesn't know where the hospital was located, but he was kept there until March 13th. German doctors operated on him several times, removing the shrapnel from his head. He was very well treated, the nuns in the hospital even having a party for him on his birthday. There were no other Allied prisoners in this hospital and no one spoke English. Finally, as the Allies were getting close to the hospital, he was taken to a railway station and put in a box car with straw, for the three day trip to Fällingbostel and Stalag XIB, the prison camp where he was reunited with Bob and his Essex Scottish friends.

To return to Bob's entry in his diary:

I was taken to the German Divisional Head Quarters for

questioning and travelled around to a few other places in one of those fancy German touring cars. I was seated in the back seat (in style) and, when I realized that I was still alive and wasn't going to be shot, I relaxed somewhat and pulled out my cigarette package to have a smoke. The German officers indicated that they would like a cigarette too—so I gave each of them one cigarette, and put the package back in my pocket! They also gave me a piece of German sausage which I couldn't eat because of the smell (and how I dreamed of that later!)

The next day I was taken to a sort of headquarters for more questioning. The officer questioning me there spoke excellent English, had gone to university in the States and said to me "Don't you people know you should be fighting with us against the Reds?" Here there was lots of activity—officers in their high polished boots coming and going and lots of saluting and "Heil Hitlers!" It was just like in the movies, with candles stuck in wine bottles—the works! [It is entirely possible that Bob was in the company of the famous Heinz Guenther Guderian! Undoubtedly, Bob's interrogators were planning their attack against the allied lines.] *He also seemed surprised that I was "just" a lance corporal when I had been at university. I said that I wondered about that, too! Of course, under the Geneva Convention, as a prisoner of war I was only required to state my name, rank and serial number, which I did. Of course they had my Army pay book so knew a lot about me. My captors, in English, asked me questions about my outfit—our military plans, everything, and my answer was the same— my name, rank and serial number. There was no intimidation or threat of torture. Then they seemed to forget about me—and I sat down in a corner of the room. There was a lot of discussion in German among the officers and one of them noticed me sitting there and said "Do you understand German?" With a sort of devil-may-care attitude I said "Oh, a little". As you know, Mom and Pop - I don't know any German at all—never took it in school. Then the officer said—and now everyone was listening—"Just how much German do you know?" With a straight face, and looking right at my captors, I said "Ich liebe dich"* [This means "I love you", and is the only German expression Bob knew, but his pronunciation was so bad that it probably sounded like "Ick leebey dick"]. *This broke them up. They laughed until they cried, and I joined in. I'm sure they will tell the story of that stupid Canadian to their children and grand-children in the years to come!*

After that we were marched several miles away from the front. Walked all day and slept that night in a barn with some other prisoners. About 100 of us—English and Canadians (of other regiments as well as ours). It was pretty crowded and the odour was pretty bad, but we were tired and actually slept. The wet straw and manure smell stuck with us for weeks. The next day we walked to a Transit camp at Essen (about 30 km) where we arrived at 2 a.m. where I was kept for 2 1/2 weeks. The rest were sent on, but I was kept—why I don't know even now. Had no Red Cross here and thus things were pretty grim. All my possessions were taken, except my watch, which I hid in my pant leg. Got 1/6 of loaf of bread and soup (water and a couple of potatoes with barley occasionally) a day. Never had any soap or shaving equipment, so I acquired a beauty of a beard—as well as a good coating of dirt.

Left there about March 6 or so. Marched to a station where they loaded us into three of those little European freight cars—50 in one—wounded and guards in another—and I was in one with 72 others. Spent three days and four nights in this car and I'll never forget it. There was not enough room for everyone to sit down, and the men, many of them wounded, were beginning to panic after several hours of standing. [Bob didn't tell his parents about the part he played during this—undoubtedly his worst—experience of the war. He told his family many years later that it appeared that no-one was in charge. So he shouted for attention and when he could be heard he said "*We can't all sit down at once. Everyone move to this end of the car—stand close together. Now there is a little space at the far end of the car. The first three rows can sit down. I have a watch and you can sit for 2 hours. Then you can stand up and the next few rows can sit down*". This they continued to do for the three days and four nights of this terrible trip.] *We managed to survive—but only barely. We were not allowed to leave the train at any time, even when stopped all day long. We had no water and no ventilation. There were no sanitary facilities (other than a small pail) and many of the boys were sick—both ways. Had 2/3 of loaf of bread and a small piece of sausage for the three days. Our car wasn't strafed by aircraft, so we were very lucky there. The cars in front of us were, and there were some casualties. We didn't look forward to the nights very much! We were a sorry looking mess when that trip was over and if I were in the army of occupation I know what I'd like to do—just exactly what they did there to us!*

This was the only time Bob expressed any hatred of

Germans. The guards could have given the prisoners water. After those terrible three days and four nights, they arrived at Fällingbostel prison camp in Eastern Germany.

Prisoner-of-War

Fällingbostel (Stalag XI B) was located between the Weser and the Elbe rivers, about 50 km south of Hamburg. Of course its actual location was unknown to the prisoners. Here Bob was photographed and issued with the wooden identification tag which he had to wear around his neck. He brought it back to Canada with him.

On May 15th, Bob's parents received a post card written in their son's handwriting and dated March 10th. (I have added English translations for the German words).

Kriegsgefangenenpost (Prisoner of war mail)
Recovered in Germany 16.3.45-17
Stalag XI B (Prison Camp 11B)
Vor- und Zuname (name and surname): L/CPL. SANDERSON. ROBT.
Gefangenennummer (Prison number): 200978
Deutschland (Germany)

Dear Mother and Dad,

Just a note to let you know I'm well and a P.O.W. (Prisoner of War) in Germany. Please don't worry about my condition or health—you know me, and I'm the same as ever. Your prayers have been with me, I know, and through my experiences I have been conscious of them and of you. I was captured late in the

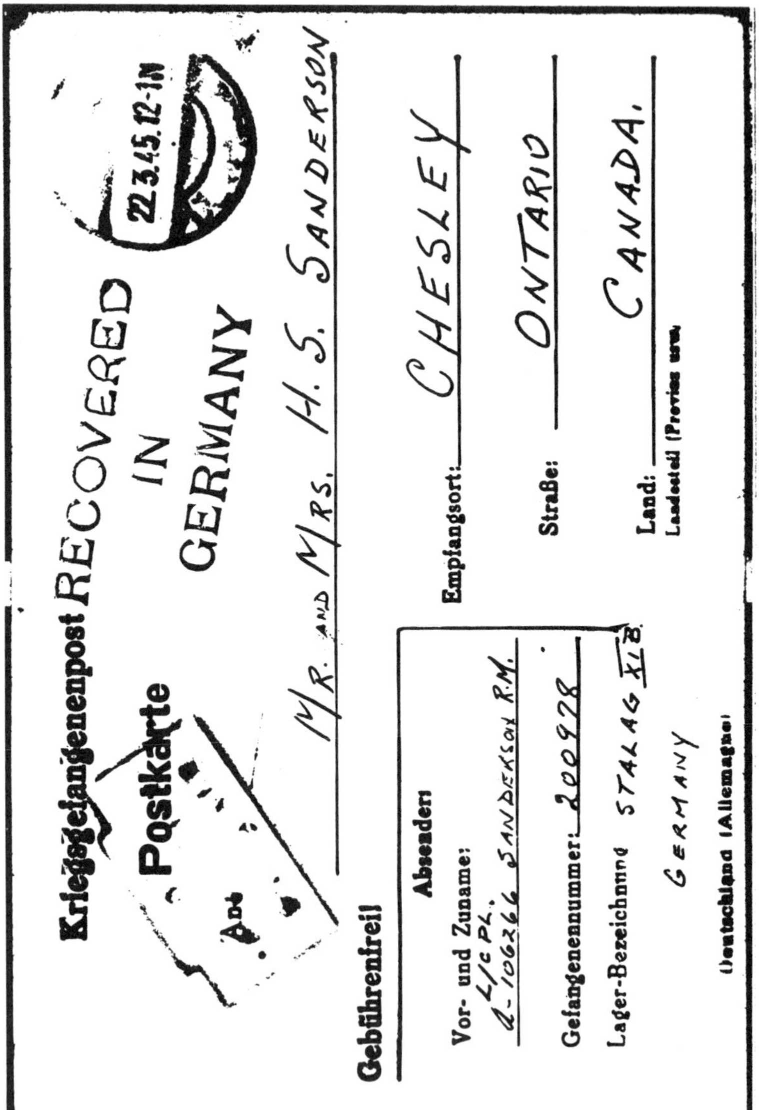

Postcard forwarded from Stalag XIB

afternoon of Feb. 19. It was rather a rough time and I ended up on the wrong side of the line when the attack was over and things were more settled. I can receive all mail sent to me and the address is on the outside of this sheet. Hope war is over before I hear from you. Hope brothers and relatives are finding things o.k. Sorry if I caused you some extra worry with the "missing" report. It bothers me very much and I do hope you get this letter. I have sent a card previous to this by a few days. Wonder if you could let Marie know? Never once thought of this ever happening to me—but that's how I've ended up. Probably belated by the time this reaches you but congratulations on celebrating one more wedding anniversary. Often think of you all and am sending much love to you two particularly. All for now and will write again as soon as possible.

Your army son—Bob

Stalag XI B was one of many German prisoner-of-war camps, and became famous after the war as the setting for the movie ***The Little Red Hen of Stalag 11B***. Like other prison camps, it was enclosed by a 9 foot high barbed wire fence with a second 6 foot high fence inside. Three feet inside the second fence there was a trip wire about 1 foot above the ground, and any prisoner who stepped over this wire was shot. There were machine gun towers at intervals around the perimeter. The camp was divided into sections for the different prisoner nationalities. The prisoners were housed in long wooden huts. Each hut had a single wooden table and food had to be eaten standing up. The bunks were usually in three tiers and some had wood-shaving mattresses. Each morning the prisoners were awakened by the guards shouting "Raus" (out) for the morning roll call when they were counted. This often took a very long time and was very hard on the prisoners in the cold winter weather.

Stalag XI B was bursting at the seams when Bob arrived, since, because of the advancing Russian army, many prisoners from camps in the eastern part of Germany had been transferred to Fällingbostel. Among these were many of the Canadians captured at Dieppe. In his book about the Dieppe prisoners, ***"Forgotten Heroes"***, Mellor wrote the following about the camp at Fällingbostel.

> *"It was a nightmare, wet, muddy and filthy . . . Food was practically non-existent, and the life-saving Red Cross parcels had not been issued for a long time . . . As winter closed its grip around the compound, conditions deteriorated. There was little fuel: the huts were miserably cold. Gradually, under the starvation diet, the flesh began to wither and shrink on their bones, so the prisoners had little or no resistance to the intense cold. Tuberculosis, bronchitis and rheumatism became rampant throughout the camp, and although the small British medical staff fought desperately to save men, the mortality rate climbed rapidly.*
>
> *In mid winter they were informed that their single blankets and mattresses would be taken away.*

> *If conditions had previously been miserable, now they became intolerable. At night, they were forbidden to leave the huts to relieve themselves. To make sure they didn't, savage doberman pinscher dogs freely roamed the compound each night . . . How long could the Canadians at Fällingbostel be expected to hold out before dying of starvation and illness?"*

This was the prison camp to which Bob arrived in early March, where he was photographed, given a number and a wooden identification tag with only the word Stalag 11B etched in the wood. He was allowed to write a second postcard to his parents on March 17, but it was never mailed. It was recovered by the Allied troops when Germany was invaded and was finally received by his parents on May 15. Of course he was not permitted to say anything about conditions in the Stalag.

Stalag XI B, Germany
March 17/45

Dear Mother and Dad,

Just a card again to let you know everything is fine and am managing very well. Hope you have heard that I am a P.O.W. while I'm writing this. Am not expecting to receive mail from you, but you can write anyway just in case I'm still here. Hope it won't be long till I'll be with you all again. Look after yourselves. Am impatient for that homecoming dinner. Regards to rest of Sandersons and relatives.

Love to Both

The mail service from Germany to the rest of the world was undoubtedly unpredictable during the last months of the war and Bob's letters were only "recovered" by the Allies in Germany after the prison camp had been liberated. However, conditions in the Stalag were described to his parents in a later letter written from England.

Marched into Stalag XI B. near Fällingbostel in the province of Hanover in the morning of March 9th at 11 a.m. Some of men I knew were here. Slept on floor for 1 1/2 weeks. Had one blanket. Very cold and drafty and rats were rather bold and a bit on the large side.

All the Canadians moved into one barrack—400 or so in one section. Slept on boards—cleaner. Some were still on floor.

Some Yank P.O.W.'s, British, Indian, etc. as well as R.C.A. and P.O.W.'s came in at end of March after 600 and 800 km. marches across Germany from Stalags overtaken by Russians. Some were in wretched condition, others were amazingly good.

Now I'm in charge of 28 men in a section, for rations, etc. Skillet better after April 1st. Heaton was brought in Easter Sunday. Looked well and said he received all possible attention. Is deaf in one ear and blind in one eye. Still miraculous. Best news so far for my morale was seeing him looking so well again.

In the Stalag things were pretty grim at times (most of the time) but we managed ok. Food was the worst problem for us. We were always hungry and thought only of food, home and end of war or liberation. The Jerries appeared to be trying to starve us and by the rations we were receiving, there's no doubt they were. There was no food in the mornings. In the afternoon we'd get 1/7 of a loaf of bread with a spoonful of sugar (maybe). Sometimes they'd favour us with some margarine. Later on they gave us 1/4 bowl of soup (water with a couple of slices of turnips). That was our usual ration with two small potatoes. We'd stretch this food out as long as possible over the day. In the mornings, usually I walked up and down the compound with a companion and we talked of our favourite foods, beginning with breakfast and going through the day. This would occupy about a half hour! I tried to walk with different people, so I could hear about different types of food. But after this, our knees would become so weak we spent the rest of the morning in bed.

We lived for the Red Cross parcels. After the first three weeks (when we hadn't any) we averaged one every ten days, to be divided among four men. Without these, we probably would have starved. After the food in the parcel was divided (my job) some of the men kept it and made bread puddings, using the raisins or chocolate with their bread ration. I got to be pretty good at dividing a raisin into three pieces! This could take a whole day and was the topic of endless banter! "How is your pudding Mrs. Jones?" "Who are you inviting for dinner, Mrs. Smith?" The prisoners made little fires in the compound to heat their food, or make their puddings. They often used boards from their bunks for firewood.

Since I was an N.C.O., I had to look after the division of rations for 28 men, and believe me, that was a job! I never thought I'd see men fight over bread (the largest piece) and it wasn't pleasant. I finally figured out a way to avoid fights. The men turned their backs after I had divided the bread and I pointed to a piece of bread and asked "whose is this?" And in turn they gave a name. [Actually, without knowing it, Bob was using the same system as some other starving men had used, those men with the Scott Antarctic expedition who spent the winter of 1912-13 in a cave in the snow in the Antarctic!]

I was never man-handled by Jerry guards, but I saw others who were. Never saw them shoot a prisoner but reports came to us of them doing it. I had gone three weeks without cigarettes so I traded some of mine for bread. Almost sold my watch for 60 cigarettes to get food, but figured if others could get by on the rations— I could—so I still have it. Many sold their watches and rings for cigarettes, which were then traded with the guards for food. [In all the prison camps there were some soldiers who excelled in trading. Cigarettes were the medium of exchange and these were used by the traders to barter with the German guards for food].

The conditions in the camp were pretty awful. I slept on the floor and used a brick with my gloves over it for a pillow. The last couple of weeks I scored a wooden bed and had one blanket. Jerry took our leather jackets, so it was a bit cool at night. There was no water so we couldn't wash, and we got pretty filthy. Of course, we had no clothes except our uniforms, so we couldn't take these off. My underwear finally disintegrated, and with the dirty clothes, everybody got body lice. Most of the camp had dysentery and things were a bit on the filthy side. The lavatories broke down soon after I arrived, and a large outdoor "bleacher" structure was erected in the compound and used as a lavatory. You can imagine the smell! I was sick for about a week, but wasn't as bad as many of the others.

About once or twice a week each of us Canadians had to go out pulling stumps for wood. Those were grim mornings on an empty stomach. We were all so weak we were plenty tired after the long walk back. It was at least exercise for us, and it really did us more good than harm. [Bob never mentioned in his letter, since perhaps he was unaware, that according to the Geneva Convention, officers and NCOs who were prisoners of war could not be forced to work. However, in those days in that Stalag it would have been useless to complain. And there were some good things about getting outside the Stalag walls. Many years later, Bob recalled that on one such stump–pulling day when he was returning to the Stalag at the rear of the group of prisoners, a German farmer with a cart load of potatoes came up behind him. He motioned for Bob to take some potatoes from the cart, which of course, Bob was happy to do, filling his pant legs with potatoes. With his pant legs bulging with potatoes he waddled into camp. They had no fire, but the prisoners in Bob's section were happy to eat the potatoes raw, like apples!]

While in the Stalag, the most I ever saw in a funeral

procession was nine. Always one or two a day. Usually wounded men or others who died of malnutrition. There were about 8000 in our Stalag counting all the nationalities. No doubt you've seen pictures of Belsen camp. Our camp was laid out similarly, but thank goodness our camp wasn't for political or Jewish prisoners! They were terrible!

Such conditions certainly bring out the true personality of men and there's where you find out what a person is really like. As I said before it teaches you to appreciate the simpler things of life and almost tends to take away ambition—just to have a satisfied stomach and a home was about all you'd wish for then.

Well, this has turned into quite a catalogue, but thought I should tell you a few things that happened—because I know how interested you are. There's lots more to say, but I've got to have something to talk about when I get home—don't I?

The last letter Bob wrote from the prison camp (dated April 20), took a month to arrive in Chesley, but at least his parents knew that he had survived prison life! Stalag XI B had been liberated, but the prisoners were still there.

Fri., April 20/45 (Received May 20/45)

Dear Mother and Dad,

I am writing this while still in our old home—Stalag XI B—the German Prison camp, but under much different conditions as you have learned by now, I hope. We were liberated by the British Army on April 16th and although we have been free men for a couple of days, we are still very exuberant and not quite used to it as yet.

It was quite a day and one I shall never forget. Some of the boys have been prisoners for quite a few years and when our tanks finally arrived at the gates and the Jerries disarmed, they were overcome with joy. Will have lots to tell you.

Oh yes! In case you were wondering, I am very well and have no ill effects from my new experience in "Jerrieland". I've probably lost rather a few of my excess poundage, but I always did have a fair surplus to work on, so there's no harm there. I guess a little starvation is good, because I feel excellent. [Bob never told his parents that he had lost 50 pounds from his 170 pound frame. Actually, he was not very well for several months after liberation, and the chronic dysentery he contracted in the prison camp remained with him the rest of his life].

It is hard to say just what will become of me—that is—where I'll end up. But it is rather definite that we'll be in England very shortly. The conditions here are slightly on the disagreeable side, particularly from the sanitary viewpoint and the authorities are trying to get us out as soon as possible. Some have left, but they are prisoners of priority such as wounded, sick and "Kriegies" (prisoners of war—German word) of up to five years and should leave first. Rumour has it that they are being flown to their destination so I am hoping it is a true rumour for once.

Another rumour is that I may be home very soon, so I'm keeping my fingers crossed and hoping for that too!

Have been wondering how everything is back home—how you are and how Art and Hardie are looking after their respective services. Boy, what a day when we're all together again and it doesn't seem very far away now!

All for now. Remember me to all and Aunt Flo and Uncle Jim. Have written a few cards from here to you all, but don't imagine they'll ever reach home. This is quite a bit more dependable service than the Jerries can produce.

Much love and I'll try and give you an address to write to soon.

Love -

Back to England

Bob's next letter to his parents was from a hospital in England. How wonderful it was to be liberated from the prison camp, to be clean and well-fed, to hope to be soon sent home to Canada.

Tues. May 1/45

Dear Mother and Dad,

How I have been wondering about you two and all! I think I have an address now that should get me. I arrived in England on Fri. April 27 by air. It was a wonderful non-stop flight and took only from 2 p.m. till 5.30 for the trip. Wish I could tell you all about it, but hope to soon. Have been treated royally since leaving the Stalag XI B in Germany and they appear as if they can't do enough for us. Landed at a British reception centre airport then went to the main reception camp. Sure is great to be back in England and act like a human being again! Saturday travelled by train and truck to #4 Canadian General Hospital where I am at present. Am sure you are wondering about me, but for goodness sakes, I hope you aren't worrying about me any more. I am at the hospital for observation or convalescence or re-outfitting. The out-fitting is all I need and expect to go on a 14 day leave by the end of this week. I lost a few pounds, but other than that I'm as fit as I was last summer. I am more fortunate than others but I always did have a real constitution thanks to my up-bringing! We're all being given a complete medical and x-rays, etc., just in case, and our special diet—which consists of 6 meals a day of the most delectable food the army can give. Used to dream of such meals! It's a wonderful life I'm having now. The Red Cross has certainly won my respect both while in the Stalag and while returning here as well as here in the hospital. No one knows quite what will happen to us at present. May go home (too wonderful to think of) or may stay here in England for awhile—but what ever it is I'm not worrying about it at present for we'll all be home soon. The war can't be going very much longer now! (By the way—I still don't like ONIONS!!! Amazing eh!)

All my personal belongings were taken by Jerry so I have no addresses at all—can't even remember the name of Jeff's wife, however, I'm sure I'll manage and find some of our friends over here.

Do hope I hear from you soon and learn your news. This is my first letter from England. Sent you flowers to-day for mothers day.

Love,

Fri. May 4/45

My dear mother and dad,

Am thinking of you two very much these days and I wish I could just even talk to you on the phone but the Atlantic is quite a width for that and priorities are always present—however, I can write you and it sure feels grand to be able to do that once more. This is my 3rd airmail I believe since I was liberated so I hope you have received them alright. Hope you both are well. I know you mother and you too dad, only you don't show it as much, openly, but you've both had quite a worry about me and it's bothered me very much - knowing I was safe and in a prison camp and yet not sure you'd ever received that news. I do hope it reached you before my cablegram arrived. Through it all over here and in fact everywhere, I knew your prayers were with me. I seemed to feel it —particularly Feb. 19—when I had time to think back over it all later. Hope you have had someone home during these rather glum looking days when you didn't know the story about me.

Well, it looks like the war in Germany is practically over. By the time this reaches you, it should be, so whether I get home as an X-P.O.W. or not, it looks like we'll all be home very soon. I'm still at #4 hospital but I am hoping for my release papers to-morrow and then my 14 day leave to see things and live a bit again. First holiday since leaving Canada and I'm looking for-ward to it. I've had my medical (to-day) and I'm still A-1—what else could I be—eh? I have a few souvenirs of Germany, and I'm going to send them to you sometime soon when I get a chance.

Have seen a few shows at Aldershot and sure enjoyed them —good or not. Was talking to Bill Neilson (Stratford) at one show. Good to see him. He's looking well now and waiting to go home. Had been wounded in Belgium. Also was talking to Gordon Reid of our district and got a little news of Chesley. Great to see some-one from home. Expect to get some Enterprises from him soon.

I've gained about 10 lbs since I was liberated—I'm going to have to watch myself from now on—but the meals they serve us (double rations) are indescribable and strictly not G.I. Most of the boys have improved 100%. We used to dream of these meals by the hour a few weeks ago. One thing I've learned out of my new experience, ma, is to appreciate the "simple things of life" more than ever before. So everything has its good part for you somewhere.

Jerry took everything including my address book, so I'm at a bit of a loss there. I hid my watch down my pant leg and luckily he missed it when he searched me—so I still have that anyhow. Send me a few pictures—I haven't one of anybody and I'd sure love to look on my ma and pa's countenances.

Thought I'd tell you that I've got a gorgeous moustache grown in Germany. You'd like it, I know.

Much love -

On May 7, 1945, at Rheims in France, all German forces surrendered unconditionally. The war in Europe was over! At this date, there were 282,000 Canadian men and women in army uniform in Europe. The Army's casualties numbered 74,374 of whom 22,964 died. Bob told his parents of the VE day celebrations in London.

Sunday, May 14/45
Glasgow, Scotland

Dear Mother and Dad,

Have been intending to write sooner than this since starting my leave but you can imagine how difficult that is with all the excitement that has been going on over here recently. I left on my leave last Saturday and went to London. Visited there and saw the sights and when "V" day came I was still there. It was a glorious day for people over here and they celebrated the day in no uncertain manner. I was with the crowds around Trafalgar Square, Piccadilly and Buckingham Palace, but unfortunately, was there just at the wrong time to see the Royal Family and Churchill. Thursday night I took the train to Glasgow where I am now. I got in touch with Beth and Friday we got together and did a bit of visiting I and got some news of home [Bob's Stratford cousin, Beth Preston, was a navy nurse stationed near Glasgow. She has since told me how shocked she was when she first saw Bob, with only 120 pounds on his 6 foot frame. He was able to eat only a very little at a time, so they joked that he had to have 5 or 6 meals a day. He also had sores in his mouth, and his hair was falling out, she remembers]. *It was wonderful seeing her and she's looking well, I must say. Also told me that you'd got word of my safety and I feel so much better about it all now. Saturday Beth and I went on a boat trip through the different lochs and had a grand day. Saw hilly Scotland and a glimpse of famous Loch Lomond. I like Scotland better than England too as do many other Canadians over here.*

Beth says you both are well. I've caused you a great deal of worry but I know you both would be wonderful about it. This is Mothers Day, and I'm thinking of you to-day, ma and wish I could be with you.

Hope my flowers got to you in time for to-day. There's no better girl in this world, than you mom, and I sure wish I were home to-day to tell you so. Been wondering about you too Dad so I'll end up with sending lots of love to you both and hope to see you soon.

Love from your son

Bob was still hoping that as an ex-prisoner of war, he might be sent home soon, but this was not to be. Repatriation was on a "point" basis, and since the army didn't give him extra "points" for his time in the Stalag, he had to reconcile himself to remaining in England.

Tuesday, May 22nd/45

Dear Mother and Dad,

I've just returned from my wonderful 16 day leave and I'm back on army depot once more. Last place I wrote to you was Glasgow I think. I stayed there for six days. The people were very good to me and I have a very good impression of the Scottish people—better than the English. My last four days weren't too pleasant since I was a little under the weather but am feeling fine again. Think it was my stomach and tired out. There's no doubt, civilization is hard on you, but it's wonderful when you get used to it again.

Well, coming back to a camp was just like going home—I was hoping for home letters and I wasn't disappointed. I just got my first mail and I scored letters from you and lots of friends. Boy, you've no idea how wonderful it was to hear from you again. I do hope my letters have been reaching you ok now. I've re-read your letters and the others several times already. I've caused a lot of unpleasantness and worry for you all and will have to get home soon and make up for it. As far as I know, I'll be around for a while yet. Men are returning to Canada under a point basis and my total is rather low in comparison. My six months in Holland and Germany aren't going to make a great deal of difference which doesn't seem fair, however, I'll have to wait my turn and it shouldn't be long. I'm hoping for Inverhuron this summer.

Mary McCulloch's patient was Frank Chauvin, my Company Commander and tops in men. You mentioned Pete Heaton and writing his family. Pete was with me and it's a long story but he ended up very badly wounded about the face but showed up at Stalag XI B later on. He has a few scars, blind in one eye and deaf in one ear, but it is really miraculous. I thought he was a goner when I patched him up. I wouldn't tell his mother about all this. He's looking very well considering everything and after his operations should be as good as ever. Don't think he told his parents that he was wounded.

I don't like thinking about what happened to me but it's an experience I should share with others and at least tell my two bosses about anyway. It sometimes appears to be a long time ago, but other times it's always in my mind. However, it's all past now and I'm still very glad that I joined the infantry and particularly that I belong to the Essex Scottish Regt. I fought with some of the best boys I've ever met and why I came through while many of them didn't I'll never know or understand.

Later (I'm continuing this letter after I had a little rest). Liberation day was a wonderful day at Stalag XI B. We saw the front line Jerries retreating past our camp and then the British tanks of the 7th Armoured Corps came up 1/2 hour later. Some of the prisoners of four years or more just wept and couldn't believe it. I was a bit boisterous myself as we cheered the boys by. Didn't take us long to break through the barbed wire and be really outside and free. We began looting the S.S. barracks across from our camp the next day. They had tons and tons of food stored in some of the warehouses—enough to feed thousands for months—so we really stacked up with sugar, porridge, rice, soup, flour, barley, potatoes, carrots, and chickens (roosters too). We were all quite sick for about several days till we ate more sensibly, but it was wonderful anyway. When they gave us white bread once more, it was just like candy.

We also looted the Quartermaster's stores and got hundreds of fountain pens, lighters, pouches, pipes, wallets, etc. Also got two camouflaged sniper jackets and will send them home soon. I found a small diary and wrote in it before we left camp. Here are some notes from those wonderful days.

"April 20

Had another bowl of mush to-day for breakfast—wonderful. Have bags of sugar! Still quite a few sick with G.I.'s, influenza, tonsillitis and general overeating.

Having a hard time keeping the bugs and lice in check during this hot weather. Everyone is sitting in the sun trying to catch the little bastards.

"Monty" is expected to-morrow. Hope he gets us out of this disease infested hole soon. A pay parade was arranged and I drew 200 German Invasion marks, so now I have money again.

Am feeling stronger in the knees these days so I guess the good "compo" rations are doing a good job. Have finished my vitamin pills and they really make a difference.

Friday April 21

Had wonderful breakfast. Have dreamed of it often—bowl of mush, sausage, toast, jam and coffee. Couldn't eat it all which was disgusting, but it sure was good.

"Monty" here to-day. Gave us a short talk and inspected our barracks and looked over the conditions. He should have high boots for such a job!!! The humourous side of the situation was that while he was on a raised platform addressing the troops, the whole platform collapsed—but it never phased General Montgomery who continued his address!

Rumour that some of us (Canadian) may move out to-morrow—those captured before the 20th of February. I made it by one day, so here's hoping!

<u>*Sunday April 22*</u>

Thirty-one prisoners are heading for England to-morrow. Maybe Tuesday for me. Saw R.A.F. stage show. Entertaining in spots but musical selections were all good—orchestra and all. Also saw "Mr. Lucky" with Cary Grant and Lorraine Day. Enjoyed it very much. Never missed a woman in XI B, till I saw one in this picture!!! One thing I've learned is that when there's neither food nor women—you miss food and forget about women. Our talk was always of food and home—never girls! The men must be feeling better for I noticed a change in the conversation to-day!

<u>*Monday April 23*</u>

Socks are practically "Kaput", rotting on my feet. Hope we get some clean clothes soon. [It had been more than two months since Bob had had a shower or a change of clothes]. *No men leaving to-morrow—31 went to-day. Saw another show—musical with several big name orchestras. Was a treat!*

My tongue and mouth inside are covered with small sores and I can't eat or taste my food. Probably from my stomach not being used to the food—and too much sugar and cigarettes.

The Russians in the camp went almost wild in their new freedom. They carried in bags full of food every day. Don't know what they did with it. They couldn't possibly have eaten it all.

One day I took a walk to have a look at the cemetery up on the hill with an English friend. It was quite a sight. There must have been 20,000 buried on that hill. There were big square plots where from 8 to 100 were buried with no marks or stones to tell who was there. There were hundreds of these squares. There was one plot where comrades had erected a stone saying—"98 Belgians buried here who died accidentally". Some of the graves were well-looked after and marked—particularly the French, English and Canadian ones.

Thursday April 26th

A big day for us. Took my personal belongings (loot) and with the other 64 Canadians left camp. Was placed in charge of one group of 30 for our plane.

Arrived in transit camp at 3 p.m. Eighty of us to a tent for the night.

The drive through Germany was very interesting. It is a beautiful country—if only they knew how to look after it administratively. Roads are fair and busy with large Allied conveys. Saw many civilians, some looking dejectedly at us—others trying to fraternize. White flags flying at front of every house.

Many battlefields passed along the way and graves of both sides seen along the sides of road.

Friday April 27

Wonderful meals! Went by transport to air field 40 miles from Bremen—short ride from camp. All types of planes here. Area badly bombed, but runways are in good shape, naturally. Piled on our Dakota with all R.C.A.F. crew and left at 2 p.m. in a heavy rain. Was a smooth trip and a wonderful experience [it was Bob's first airplane ride]. *Could look out windows and see the ground when the clouds weren't too thick. Had run of ship and even got into the cockpit. Listened to movie over ear-phones for some time. Enjoyed whole trip immensely. Passed over Brussels.*

Europe looks very picturesque from air with all its canals and wandering rivers and roads. Fields of all shapes, sizes and colours and the towns and cities among them made the greatest sights! Can see how bombing could be done and how a train would be strafed. Can also see why the boys like to fly. One experience is enough to see why! It's perfect, and our trip was uneventful as far as danger goes. Looked over English channel and could see a few ships. Little bumpy over England. Looked over massive London and then had a perfect landing at Wing 40, N.W. of London, at 5.30 p.m. Walked over to a large hangar and was deloused (welcome to England!) [Bob later said it was an embarrassing situation. The ex-prisoners were squirted with delousing powder, then their clothes removed and all were given showers. Next came another examination and those still with body lice—Bob was one—were squirted again and their body hair shaved. Only then did they receive clean uniforms!] *After a short medical to see if all was ok, they brought us to a table for a lovely lunch. Grand reception! Hangar decorated and good morale booster there. Went by truck to English reception centre and had a grand meal as soon as we arrived. Went to a dance at night and had wonderful time."*

And then continuing with the letter:

One thing that always bothered me very much is how things were at home. I hated to think of the report back home and what you two must have been going through and yet I could do nothing about it.

I see the rain has stopped so I think I'll go for a "wee" stroll. The sun is shining now and you'd hardly know it had rained except for the wet streets. It's a funny climate over here—pleasant one hour and really dismal the next.

Much love -

And then for Bob it was back to the old army routine and waiting and hoping for transport home. But there were thousands of soldiers, sailors, airmen, to repatriate and not many ships to carry them. Bob complained in a letter on June 18th.

Sunday June 18/45
"Beaver Club", London

Dear Mother and Dad,

I'm on a week end to-day and in London again. Since writing to you last I've been moved to #3 training battalion and there I will probably stay until I head for home. I am very disgusted with the way things are over here, and the way we are being shoved around. It appears that they are trying to make it so uncomfortable for us that we'll end up joining up for Burma and thus get home sooner and at least out of this situation. Many are doing just that and I'm going to be one of them soon—but I haven't succumbed as yet (I'm used to taking quite a bit). Our camp is a mess and it's miles from everywhere although London is only about 25 miles or so away, and all we do is guard duty and fatigues and I think I'm entitled to a better army life than that. However, I'm not alone in my story. At one time back in the prison camp I thought I'd never complain about anything as long as I got out, but this jolt back to real army treatment after the way we were looked after over here is taking a little while to stomach properly. Unless I volunteer for Burma it appears as if I'll be here for quite a few months. So—I'm not very happy to-day. There is no one in the camp I've known personally and I've got to make new friends again. Some of the boys I knew have been sent to other camps of different military districts.

Well, this hasn't been a particularly nice letter, but thought I'd tell you about how I feel anyway—and I feel better now, just telling you.

Hope I'm in a better mood when I write next time. Should have postponed this one till I felt better. Not right to send letters full of trouble—but I'll be very disappointed if I don't get home and see you all soon and get to Inverhuron this summer. Well, all for now—

Much love your army son

Epilogue

It soon became evident that Bob would not be in Canada that summer of 1945, since there were thousands of service men waiting for transport back to Canada, and repatriation was based on a point system. There were many soldiers who had been in Europe for years, so they were given passage before Bob. He had to resign himself to the thought of remaining in England for a while.

Wed. June 13/45
#3 C.I.T.R., C.A.O.

Dear Mother and Dad,

Have just returned from my second 14 day leave and am trying to accustom myself to army routine once again. I can't say that I am enjoying it here at all, however I'm hoping that I won't have to put up with it much longer. It is still very indefinite what is in store for me until my turn comes for a Canada-bound voyage. I can't return to my regiment now nor can I be used in the army of occupation. I can volunteer for the Japan war, but I understand they have plenty of volunteers at present and I'm just biding my time until I get home. If I can be discharged I'm ready for it. I think I've had enough travelling around and experiences to do me for awhile and it's time I got busy at my future—but if I'm not discharged when I return—I'll go to the other war.

The army, as far as I'm concerned, has given me some unforgettable experiences, lots of travelling and new friends, which I value. It's a valuable experience and I would never have missed it for anything, but now that it's past, it's time for me to think of what lies ahead and I'm still wondering just what I'll do with myself. That occupies most of my thoughts once more. I never had those thoughts when I was on the continent, but I have to face them now and decide once and for all what I am going to do with my life.

You've had your share of troubles and I'm sorry circumstances made me another of your worries. However, summer is coming and I'm sure all the clan is looking forward to Inverhuron..

Lots of love -

As Bob indicated in the June 13th letter, he had had enough of army life and he didn't want to volunteer for the Pacific war. If he had done so, he would have been sent home immediately for leave before going to the Pacific and of course, would not have had to go since the war in the Pacific was over in August.

However, there was no way he wanted any more war experience. He never mentioned the killing to his parents and it was something he never wanted to talk about. Just once he admitted that on that fateful February day, he had killed quite a few German soldiers. Pinned down in the slit trench, and seeing his friends killed had triggered an unbelievable rage at the enemy and an urge to retaliate. But after his years in the army, he would never again take up a weapon to kill anything, and could never understand hunting as a sport.

Since he did not volunteer for the Japanese war, he was obliged to stay in the army in England until the spring of 1946. He was assigned work in an education unit stationed in the Brylcreem factory which was (and still is) situated near the M-4 highway from London to Heathrow airport. He even managed a trip to Paris, fulfilling his hope during his life in the trenches of seeing France. He finally returned to Canada in April, 1946, but not to a hero's welcome. The war had been over for almost a year and people wanted to forget the war and get on with their lives.

And perhaps those months in England were necessary for him psychologically. He wasn't sure of his future and what he wanted to do. His original goal of a career in medicine had changed since he had seen enough of suffering and death. He was interested in the health field and finally decided on a career in dentistry. Also, because of his army experience and being ordered about, and told what to do, what to wear, even what to eat, he decided that he would choose a career where he was his own boss. The idea of dentistry thus appealed to him and on returning to Canada, he was accepted into dental school at the University of Toronto. We were married in the summer of 1946 just before he began his university studies in September of that year.

Upon graduation in 1950, he decided to set up his dental practice in Windsor. His choice was due partly to the fact that his Uncle Hardie was a medical doctor there, but also because he felt a special fondness for Windsor because of the Essex Scottish regiment.

During the first few years of our married life, Bob often

had nightmares when he would awaken drenched with sweat. His worst nightmares were of that battle on February 19th and the terrible train ride to the prison camp. But he was fond of telling our children about his war experiences. On trips to the family cottage at Inverhuron, still Bob's favourite place in all the world, he would entertain the children with his army stories. Mostly he told of the humorous incidents and the children's favourite was the "Ich liebe dich" one. Often, too, on cold winter nights he would reminisce *"Can you imagine digging a hole out on our lawn and spending the night there? What a crazy thing to do"*.

He went to the Essex Scottish reunions and enjoyed reliving the war with Frank Chauvin, while he was still alive, with Pop Goggins and especially with Pete Heaton. Pete became the postmaster in Harrow and, although not in the best of health, is still alive today.

On trips to Europe later we visited Nijmegen and Mook in Holland and the battle areas in the Rhineland, and Bob tried to find the location of that February battle near Louisendorf. We found the church near which the battle had taken place (see photo on page 161). However, he never was sure that he could recognize the actual site, saying *"They've paved the roads, the hedges have grown and my memory has faded!"* We visited Germany several times and he never harboured any ill will for Germany or the German soldiers he had encountered. He had great respect for the German "Windhund" soldiers he had fought against and especially of course for the soldiers who took him prisoner rather than shoot him on that February day. He celebrated February 19th every year as his second birthday. He often stated that the treatment of the prisoners of war worsened as the distance from the front lines increased. He could never forget the inhuman treatment of the prisoners in the cattle car, or the actions of some of the guards in Fällingbostel. He was never interested in visiting the site of the prison camp.

We also visited the Canadian cemetery at Groesbeek in Holland which is so beautifully maintained by the Dutch people. We saw the long rows of little white crosses and graves of those men (boys really) like Ed Bartholemew and Bob Sallows and others of the Essex Scottish who died in the battle of February 19th or the later Rhineland battles.

Bob wrote in his letter of June 13th that the army had given him a valuable experience which he would never have missed for anything. This may sound surprising in view of the fact that he was never given the chance for officer's training which he so wanted. He barely escaped death on February 19th, and he almost died of starvation in the German prison camp. Nevertheless, like many ex-service men of the Second World War, Bob considered himself very fortunate to have been involved in such an historic undertaking. He was proud of representing his country and doing his part in what he believed to be a just war. Without doubt, it was the most memorable experience of his life!

He lived for more than thirty years after that fateful February day and he treated each day as a gift that he had not expected to receive. He loved his family, his work, his church and his country. However, his army and prison camp experience doubtless shortened his life. He died of a heart attack when he was 56 years old.